THE CHALLENGE OF CARING

Published by
The Bible Reading Fellowship
15 The Chambers, Vineyard
Abingdon OX14 3FE
United Kingdom
Tel: +44 (0)1865 319700
Email: enquiries@brf.org.uk
Website: www.brf.org.uk
BRF is a Registered Charity

ISBN 978 1 84101 748 8
First published 2001 under the title *Never Too Old to Grow*
Revised edition published 2011
10 9 8 7 6 5 4 3 2 1 0

Acknowledgments

Unless otherwise stated, scripture quotations are taken from the Holy Bible, New International Version, copyright © 1973, 1978, 1984 by International Bible Society, and are used by permission of Hodder & Stoughton Publishers, a member of the Hachette Livre UK Group. All rights reserved. 'NIV' is a registered trademark of International Bible Society. UK trademark number 1448790.

Scriptures taken from The Revised Standard Version of the Bible, copyright © 1946, 1952, 1971 by the Division of Christian Education of the National Council of the Churches of Christ in the United States of America, are used by permission. All rights reserved.

The Living Bible copyright © 1971 by Tyndale House Publishers.

Scriptures quoted from the Good News Bible published by The Bible Societies/HarperCollins Publishers Ltd, UK © American Bible Society 1966, 1971, 1976, 1992, used with permission.

Extracts from the Authorised Version of the Bible (The King James Bible), the rights in which are vested in the Crown, are reproduced by permission of the Crown's Patentee, Cambridge University Press.

A catalogue record for this book is available from the British Library

Printed in Singapore by Craft Print International Ltd

THE CHALLENGE OF CARING

BIBLE-RELATED REFLECTIONS

ALEXINE CRAWFORD

ACKNOWLEDGMENTS

A book such as this draws on the varied experiences of many. I would like to thank all the kind people who have told me their stories, sometimes at considerable cost to themselves. The stories are true but the names have been changed.

Thanks are due also to others who have written about ageing, caring and being cared for, not least the writer of the book of Genesis.

My own parents did much to shape my outlook. Pioneers in their time, initiating the fun of camping for many disabled folk, throughout 40 years they spread the message to treat people as people, regardless of their disabilities.

Lastly, I continually thank my husband Warren for his constant support and encouragement, both keeping me anchored and giving me space.

NOTE FOR THE NEW EDITION

Over the ten years since this book was first published, I have lost count of the readers who have told me, 'This book is just what I needed.' Some have even had to reclaim their copy from the relative they were caring for!

Now, as another generation takes up the challenge of caring, I sense an additional challenge, the challenge of being cared for. From this perspective the original title, Never Too Old to Grow, *is more relevant than ever. There is always room for growth.*

CONTENTS

WHAT ABOUT ME?

FORGIVENESS

THE PERSON INSIDE

A GOOD DYING

FOREWORD

There can be little doubt that over the coming years care of the elderly is going to be of increasing importance; the NHS, voluntary organisations, social services, churches and charities must face the challenge and do so with compassion.

Alexine Crawford writes with clear-eyed honesty about the care of the elderly and brings to her task not only her own experiences but also her own particular understanding of the scriptures. The result is a book which is discomforting, a challenge—but one which all Christians have to encounter. How do we, in practical and spiritual terms, honour the elderly? And what can we do, as individuals and within society, to ensure that elderly people are treated with dignity, respect and Christ-like understanding?

This book is very timely.

The Rt Revd Christopher Herbert

INTRODUCTION

When I passed my half-century, it seemed that every other contemporary I spoke to had, as I did, an elderly relative needing care. Many problems we were facing were common to us all, though the attempted solutions varied widely. I began to ask myself what difference being a Christian made to this care.

If differences there were, they could affect every aspect, not just a sort of 'optional extra' spiritual dimension. Jesus demonstrated that how a person relates to God affects his or her inner attitudes, and those inner attitudes have practical, physical outworkings. His own loving response to his Father's promptings led him into close contact with people who were deranged, dirty, diseased, dying or even dead.

In him God's love permeated the whole of life. In him accepted negatives were overturned. 'Human nature doesn't change', the hopelessness of entrenched relationships, the apparent finality of damage to soul or body—all could be touched and transformed.

Could we also, 2000 years after Jesus' earthly life, experience such motivation? Could Jesus enter into the ordinary mess of family life and make a difference? Could he even affect relationships with an elderly relative? If he could, I wanted to know about it, to experience it. I wanted to let God have his way through ageing towards death.

In this book I relate my own discoveries, and those shared with me by friends, of what he can do and has done. These discoveries are relevant to carers of sick or disabled people of all ages, and to those looking after the elderly, and they are best summarised in Paul's words in his second letter to the Corinthians (4:16): 'Therefore we do not lose heart. Though outwardly we are wasting away, yet inwardly we are being renewed day by day.'

CHOICE—HOW IT BEGAN FOR ME

Many are the plans in the mind of a man, but it is the purpose of the Lord that will be established.

PROVERBS 19:21 (RSV)

Every way of a man is right in his own eyes, but the Lord weighs the heart.

PROVERBS 21:2 (RSV)

As an Army family, we moved every two or three years, directed by the posting department of the Ministry of Defence. The only choice of location we had, and that not always, was in the particular house we would occupy.

Other choices were plentiful as to how I would live my life, what commitments I would make, what hospitality we would give, what hobbies pursue. Returning to England to what was likely to be our last Army posting, and provided with a pleasant four-bedroomed house, I had all sorts of projects and ideas in mind. But God had other purposes to establish. He weighed my heart and saw what he wanted to bring about there, and not only there but throughout our family.

The more personal parts of the readings that follow will be easier to understand if I outline the framework in which God brought this about.

When my father died some years earlier, we were living in Germany. Our next posting brought us within a three-quarter-hour drive of my mother, who remained in the family home, now much too big for one person.

I drove over every Thursday as a daughterly duty, doing what jobs I could, trying to help with what she was finding difficult. It was not easy. Her abilities declined during those three or four years, and she began to have small imperceptible strokes—interruptions of the blood supply to the brain which gradually led to 'multi-infarct dementia'.

We felt that she needed someone actually living in the house, for her own security and for a friendly presence, so with her agreement we adapted two rooms into a tiny flat. The couple who moved in were not without their own problems but they were there, and they were friendly while respecting my mother's guarded privacy.

When they left the flat, it became the answer to another Christian couple's prayer, for only three weeks before their wedding they had had nowhere to live. By this time we were stationed in Belgium, making trips back across the Channel both for our children and to update arrangements for my mother. The couple undertook some care, but then on one of my visits they told me that they had a new job elsewhere, and that anyway they did not have the authority now needed to keep my mother clean.

I saw for myself that she was not coping with incontinence, and indeed had a sort of denial of its existence. My brother, on one visit, had run a bath for her and then heard her go upstairs and simply pull out the plug! I took her to stay for a visit with us in Belgium and bossily insisted on frequent washing to clear up her sores.

This prepared things for the lady I had quite marvellously been led to, who had some nursing experience and who moved into the flat (along with her partner) as resident carer. She was so much bossier even than I that my mother called her 'The Dragon', but she did establish a good routine.

Our final posting, with that pleasant four-bedroomed house, was just over an hour's drive from my mother's house. We arranged for our daughter's schooling, and were looking forward to establishing ourselves in this new setting when we took a week's leave to do some work in my mother's garden. On our arrival 'The Dragon', because of her partner's job, gave a month's notice.

It did not occur to us to put my mother in a home. There was a charity connected to the house for which we were partly responsible and which could not just be shelved. And the house itself, and even more its garden, meant so much to her that we saw them as necessary to her life. Because the little flat comprised part of a helper's wages, she could afford to pay for help.

I stayed with her, advertising weekly for a carer, living precariously from each issue of the local paper to the next. And then one evening as we watched television she had the only one of her mini-strokes that I ever witnessed. In those desperate moments before she regained consciousness I knew that if, with the next stroke, she died, I wanted to be with her.

Her house was roomy and my husband and three children, the eldest then aged 21, agreed to base there for the summer holidays. When the holidays ended, having failed to find anyone to share her care, I had no option but to stay on while my daughter and my husband moved back to our Army quarters, school and work, and the boys went off to university.

There seemed to be little question of choice. It might have been better to build up a team of carers, but I did not know how to do that; moreover my mother did not take easily to new people. Only after more than six months was I put in touch with someone whom my mother immediately liked, and who moved in to share her care.

A pattern developed in which my husband and daughter came over every weekend, and alternate weeks I returned with them and left the helper in charge.

Gradually my mother's abilities declined and we had to adapt accordingly. After three years, when my husband retired from the Army, we all moved into her house and the helper left. By then my mother needed total care and could no longer speak. She died a year later.

Given the option, we would never have chosen to spend those four years as we did. But there seemed to be no option, and as those years went by we realised that God was indeed accomplishing some of his purposes in and for us through it all. It became valuable and precious.

HONOUR

HONOUR

Honour your father and your mother, that your days may be long in the land which the Lord your God gives you.

EXODUS 20:12 (RSV)

'Honour your father and mother' (this is the first commandment with a promise), 'that it may be well with you and that you may live long on the earth.'

EPHESIANS 6:2–3 (RSV)

'Honour' is such an unfashionable word that you may find it as difficult to define as I did. The dictionary weaves the word in with the idea of respect (another unfashionable concept). It says that to honour is to respect highly, to confer dignity upon someone; while under 'respect' it lists 'regard with deference, esteem; avoid degrading or insulting or injuring or interfering with or interrupting; treat with consideration'.

That's a tall order! Suppose I do not feel that my parents are worth respecting? It seems, though, that the command is not to do with parents deserving respect. It is not to do with honouring those who are perfect or outstanding. Like many of God's precepts and teaching, it comes from exactly the opposite direction to our habitual viewpoint. That says 'When so-and-so shows he is worthy of respect, I will respect him', but God says that a son or daughter should honour a father or mother simply because of their parenthood, simply by virtue of their being parents.

It has nothing to do with whether they are good or bad parents, nothing to do with whether the son or daughter particularly likes them, nothing to do with whether or not the parents naturally command respect or might be thought worthy of respect. Regardless of any problems of relationship and character, and because they are your father and mother, you must honour them.

I had no problem honouring my father, a man who was respected and loved by all who knew him and of whom I was immensely proud. My mother was different. Psychologists might list all sorts of valid reasons for my negative attitude to her. God could have been much more uncomfortably probing and brought to my notice such attributes in me as jealousy, impatience, criticism, selfishness and self-regard. But he is gentle, tempering the wind to the shorn lamb and always allowing us to move slowly.

My mother was an artist with a social conscience and a lot of energy, a visionary who went straight for her objectives. Though her family was precious to her, her focus was on doing.

'What are you going to be?' she would ask a young person, meaning 'What job will you do?' rather than 'What person will you be?' She belonged to the generation of women who strove to be allowed to have a profession rather than just to be. So she could hardly believe that her daughter, despite adequate talents in various directions, had only domestic ambitions.

Five mornings a week for 20 years, Mrs Fulbrook walked up the steep bank to our house to be our 'daily woman'.

She did everything—personal washing by hand, the ironing, and all the cleaning—and in those hours she could not possibly keep the whole house spotless. For all my untidiness I disliked dirt, while I believe my mother just did not notice accumulated dust. Occasionally Mrs Fulbrook was ill, or in the autumn went hop-picking, and my mother would laugh at our different reactions.

'When Mrs Fulbrook's away,' she would say, 'I think "We'll let things slide for a bit," but Alexine says, "Good, now I can have a blitz."'

In retrospect I appreciate the way she accepted me, and wish I had learnt much, much earlier to accept her likewise. The way she always contrived to offload domestic jobs infuriated me, and my super-efficiency was often double-edged, to get things done but also to shame her. It may have shamed her, but not into doing anything, and it meant that the job was done ungraciously and did dishonour to her.

She was both shy and dramatic, and her approach to people was usually to talk about what was currently engaging her interest—a painting, the garden, or her latest library book. Often people were interested, but often too they were intimidated. She could be devastatingly, scornfully critical. I found her need for public recognition embarrassing, and did not understand the insecurities and rejections that underlay the need—nor then would I have seen any way out. I was just not her most expressive fan, rather the opposite.

Then there was her relationship to my father. There must be many people who grow up without any real understanding of the relationship between their parents. Why do they argue? Why does Mum say that? Why does Dad do this? What do they see in each other? Perhaps we only begin to glimpse the answers as we ourselves live through marriage and relationships and learn adjustments in the failures and joys.

I marvel to see little children climbing on to their daddy's knee and being cuddled, for my own father was not like that, and we never easily communicated on a personal level. Yet we had the highest regard for each other, a deep love, and a good understanding. He had very small illegible writing, yet I could usually decipher it, not because of any special skill but because I understood the way he thought.

Before I married I lived at home and worked under him in the charity for disabled people that he and my mother had founded and ran. Naturally there were sparks at times, and being self-assertive I did not always honour him, but basically we got on well. My fault was to idealise him (as I was helped to see some years later), which did not help my relationship with my mother.

My father was 17 years older than my mother. When they married, the last member of her family had just died, and the tragedies of her brothers' deaths had left her hurt and vulnerable. His desire was to make up to her for all the traumas she had suffered. At the same time he appreciated her as a companion, a sparring partner, someone of independent mind. He called her his 'cavalry subaltern', admiring her tall beauty and confidence on horseback. He saw her as an equal who none the less needed to be nurtured.

But as he grew older he needed nurturing, and neither of them found it easy to switch roles. We children—adults but yet their children—saw his struggles and her neglect. We hurt for our father and despised our mother, short on understanding and outside their situation, and were not much help to either of them about how they were feeling.

We badly needed God to show us a way out of our impasse.

DECEIVING ISAAC

One day, in Isaac's old age when he was half-blind, he called for Esau his oldest son.

Isaac: 'My son?'
Esau: 'Yes, father?'
Isaac: 'I am an old man now, and expect to die almost any day. Take your bow and arrows out into the fields and get me some venison, and prepare it just the way I like it—savoury and good—and bring it here for me to eat, and I will give you the blessings that belong to you, my first-born son, before I die.'

But Rebekah overheard the conversation. So when Esau left for the field to hunt for the venison, she called her son Jacob and told him what his father had said to his brother.

Rebekah: 'Now do exactly as I tell you. Go out to the flocks and bring me two young goats, and I'll prepare your father's favourite dish from them. Then take it to your father, and after he has enjoyed it he will bless you before his death, instead of Esau!'
Jacob: 'But mother! He won't be fooled that easily. Think how hairy Esau is, and how smooth my skin is! What

if my father feels me? He'll think I'm making a fool of him, and curse me instead of blessing me!'

Rebekah: 'Let his curses be on me, dear son. Just do what I tell you. Go out and get the goats.'

So Jacob followed his mother's instructions... Then she took Esau's best clothes—they were in the house—and instructed Jacob to put them on. And she made him a pair of gloves from the hairy skin of the young goats, and fastened a strip of the hide around his neck; then she gave him the meat, with its rich aroma, and some fresh-baked bread. Jacob carried the platter of food into the room where his father was lying.

Jacob: 'Father?'

Isaac: 'Yes? Who is it, my son—Esau or Jacob?'

Jacob: 'It is Esau, your oldest son. I've done as you told me to. Here is the delicious venison you wanted. Sit up and eat it, so that you will bless me with all your heart!'

Isaac: 'How were you able to find it so quickly, my son?'

Jacob: 'Because Jehovah your God put it in my path!'

Isaac: 'Come over here. I want to feel you, and be sure it really is Esau!'

(Jacob goes over to his father. His father feels him.)

Isaac: *(to himself)* 'The voice is Jacob's, but the hands are Esau's!'

(The ruse convinces Isaac and he prepares to give Jacob his blessings.)

Isaac: 'Are you really Esau?'

Jacob: 'Yes, of course.'

Isaac: 'Then bring me the venison and I will eat it and bless you with all my heart.'

(Jacob takes it over to him and Isaac eats; he also drinks the wine Jacob brings him.)

Isaac: 'Come here and kiss me, my son!'

(Jacob goes over and kisses him on the cheek. Isaac sniffs his clothes and finally seems convinced... As soon as Isaac has blessed Jacob, and almost before Jacob leaves the room, Esau arrives, coming in from his hunting. He also has prepared his father's favourite dish and brings it to him... Isaac begins to tremble noticeably.)

Isaac: 'Who is it who was just here with venison, and I have already eaten it and blessed him with irrevocable blessing?'

GENESIS 27:1–33 (LB, ABRIDGED)

There had been a promise from God that Jacob would be head of the family over his older twin brother Esau. But Isaac favoured Esau, and in his quiet, stubborn way determined that Esau should be the one to inherit from him. Jacob was his mother Rebekah's favourite.

Isaac and Rebekah's marriage had had problems all along. Rebekah, an impulsive and adventurous girl, had left home eagerly to marry the wealthy stranger who had so romantically sought her. She may have been disappointed that this husband, considerably older than she, was a quiet man who liked meditating in the fields of an evening, and was needing a mother-substitute as much as a wife. Childlessness was a source of tension between them until, after 20 years of marriage, the twins Jacob and Esau, rivals from conception, were born.

As the twins grew up, Rebekah found a kindred spirit in her son Jacob, who worked in the fields around the house rather than going on long hunting trips like Esau. She saw his potential—and anyway, hadn't God said he would end up on top?

Jacob and Rebekah each had their own plan to get their own way. Jacob, home-based and a good cook who prepared regular meals for himself, had once taken advantage of his brother when Esau came in from hunting, tired and hungry. He bribed him with food to hand over his birthright as elder son, a precious right in their culture, to himself the younger twin—a private transaction, of which Isaac was no doubt unaware and which Esau conveniently forgot. Anyway, the birthright was not actually negotiable; it was the father's to confirm by proclaiming a destiny and a blessing.

Now Rebekah saw her opportunity. God seemed to be leaving it very late to fulfil his promise, so she had best do it for him. She spelt out her plan, taking advantage of Isaac's blindness, of his perception of himself as old and approaching death, of the weaknesses of his nature. In the event, however, the immediate result can hardly have been what any of them had hoped. Jacob by trickery received Isaac's blessing as heir, but such was Esau's murderous disappointment that Rebekah arranged for Jacob to flee to her relations far away, conning Isaac that the purpose of his going was to find a wife. She never saw her favourite again, and Isaac had a long, blind and lonely old age.

Seeing Isaac as old and enfeebled, they did not honour him. By their actions they despised him.

DESPISING

Rise in the presence of the aged, show respect for the elderly, and revere your God: I am the Lord.

LEVITICUS 19:32

Do not despise your mother when she is old.

PROVERBS 23:22

I was shocked when God highlighted that second verse for me. The book of Proverbs was what I happened to be working through at the time, and wham! There it was.

'Yes,' I thought. 'I do despise her.' And as he gently led me to see the ways in which I despised her, and the effect this was having on our relationship, so he was able to teach me positively about what it means to honour your father and your mother.

Rebekah and Jacob's major deception of Isaac was an indication of their general attitude towards him, and could well have been the culmination of many small actions through the years, a habit of despising. Despising is most often exhibited in small things, and these can accumulate into a mindset. It is so easy not to consider a person's wishes, not to take time to consult. It is easy to scorn someone whom one does not understand.

I was visiting Jo, a dear elderly friend who, because of Parkinson's disease, could not always get her words out clearly. It was late afternoon in the hospital and two young nurses rushed into her cubicle wanting to take off her day clothes and put on her nightdress. One of them took hold of her cardigan but Jo sturdily resisted them. They urged and cajoled while her lips quivered towards words. Finally she managed to say, very quietly, 'Not in front of my visitor.' Mercifully they heard, and left her. Like many carers without good leadership and training, they had been seeing her only as an object, a task to be done in response to orders. Their approach did not recognise her dignity as a person.

In our hurry to get things done, interfering or taking things out of an old person's hands may not seem to matter very much; in fact, it might even appear as a kindness. Yet it diminishes that person. We are forgetting that, however failing their powers may be, they are still an individual whose wishes and likes and dislikes should be respected. Despising is the opposite of honouring.

There's a catch, though. The command to honour our parents does have a promise attached to it, but that promise is not 'that your father and mother may become nicer'. It is 'that your days may be long in the land which the Lord your God gives you' (RSV). Learning to honour my parents will change me—the only person I have a right or responsibility to try to change. Any change in my parents I must trust to God.

Another scripture verse came as news to me. It is found in Exodus 21:17 and Jesus quoted it. It says, 'He who speaks evil of father or mother, let him surely die' (Mark 7:9–13, RSV).

Few of us would feel that we actually speak evil of a parent, but few would deny that we complain about them at times. Those teenage moans about unreasonable restrictions, about parental unfairness, about their selfishness or even downright wickedness form a critical habit that persists into adult life. Our grievances may have been genuine: our parents may have been all those things that we complained about. Yet Jesus reiterates the command that we are not to speak evil of them. Whether or not the death penalty is physically exacted, the command suggests that disrespect to parents deeply damages the child.

It says in Deuteronomy 6:24, 'The Lord commanded us to do all these statutes… for our good always, that he might preserve us alive' (RSV). We damage not only our parents but ourselves, too, when we speak evil of them.

There are no perfect parents. Most of us have 'good enough' parents, but even they are bound to have done things that have hurt us, although we may not necessarily be aware of it. There are so many reasons for family relationships going awry—reasons of personality, reasons of circumstances, and all the baggage from past generations and relationships.

As we attempt to relate together, it is vital to try to understand one another. To do this we need to acknowledge the other person's shortcomings, the bad sides of their personality, rather than despising them or denying that any shortcomings exist.

Denying is not the opposite of despising. We might like our relations to be admirable people, good-tempered and kind. We might like to feel that our parents have always loved us, even if the evidence suggests otherwise. Yet the fact is that they are human, and the likelihood is that they will be far from perfect. We may despise them for this, or we may deny that it is so.

Denial is a wall of defence which cuts us off from help and change. A man I know so much wanted a bad parental relationship to have been good that he fantasised that it was indeed good, transferring the blame and shame on to the other parent.

One friend of mine quite evidently had considerable family problems, but she would hotly defend her parents against any suggestions of fault on their part. On the surface this might have seemed like honouring them, refusing to hear any evil against them. In reality she was burying her head in the sand. By denying the existence of problems, she was denying the opportunity to do something about them. We restrict action by God until we forgive, and you cannot forgive what you deny exists.

THE SMALL THINGS OF HONOURING

[Jesus said] 'A new command I give you: Love one another. As I have loved you, so you must love one another. By this all men will know that you are my disciples, if you love one another.'

JOHN 13:34

Love must be sincere [or genuine]. Hate what is evil; cling to what is good. Be devoted to one another in brotherly love. Honour one another above yourselves. [GNB: Be eager to show respect for one another.]

ROMANS 12:9–10

Who despises the day of small things?

ZECHARIAH 4:10

When she was in her 60s my mother was awarded the MBE. I guess, from a remark made to me some time before, that those who put her forward for the decoration had initially intended to nominate my father, for although the vision for their work for the disabled was hers, it was he who had made it possible through sustained hard work. But he, knowing that such a recognition would mean an enormous amount to her, diverted their attention to her and in due time she was summoned to Buckingham Palace.

My father, who was by then in his 80s and very lame, did not want to attend the ceremony, so my brother and I accompanied her. It was an impressive occasion. Arriving by taxi we drove right inside the palace railings and through into an inner courtyard. There an official checked our invitations and ushered us past uniformed footmen into the palace itself.

All the guests were of course dressed in their very best. Slowly we made our way up the wide and beautiful staircase, savouring our surroundings. At the top, those who were to be honoured were shown into an anteroom while the rest of us settled ourselves in the tiered seats on three sides of the throne room, a high and impressive place, rich with red carpet. In this setting, surely no one could doubt that it was an honour to be there at all, and an even greater honour to be receiving a decoration from the hand of Her Majesty.

At the appointed time, the Queen entered and stood to receive the many who filed past her to have a medal pinned to their clothes or hung around their neck. Proudly we watched our mother, looking her best in a turquoise dress and jacket, walk across the carpet with her walking stick, pause in front of the Queen, and then join the others who had been honoured. The whole event was beautifully orchestrated.

Yet, in all the magnificence, I would guess that what the majority of those who were honoured remembered of that day was not so much the pomp and splendour as the conversation they had with the Queen. This tiny, dignified, sparkling lady has the gift of being interested in people and in what they do, and she has the art of asking real questions. In the few moments she has with each, she demonstrates that that individual person supremely matters.

So it is with honouring in practice. It comes in small doses. It is about details, moments. It is about listening now to the remark that matters to the speaker now. It is about respecting a person's wishes. It is taking care in the little physical helps and comforts. It is about cultivating dignity in even the least dignified events of frail old age. It is about 'honouring one another above yourselves'. It is about taking a person seriously, as a person, as a child of God, as my parent. In a word—love.

Jesus said, 'A new commandment I give you, that you love one another.' But, we may object, isn't love an emotion? How can you command an emotion? Don't they just happen? How can we be commanded to love?

It all depends on what we understand by love. Jesus said, 'If you love me, you will keep my commandments.' And also the other way round—'If you keep my commandments, you will abide in my love.' Loving in these terms is action first and foremost. Doing the loving thing is primarily what love is. Not just what seems to be loving. Not the apparently submissive wife who says, 'Yes sir, no sir (but I'll get you in the end!)'

If it is love, the doing needs to be allied to a willingness for one's motives to be improved. The actual doing of the loving action is the start of feeling love. Even an unwillingly given kiss can overcome barriers and begin a new relationship. It says to the other person, the parent, 'Yes, you do matter.' It can thaw the coolness and rigidity of a lifetime.

In the last year of her life, my mother could not have got out of her habitual armchair even if she had had the will to do so. To give her a change of scene, as well as a change of seat, we would lift her into a wheelchair at meal times and take her into the dining room. Then, after the meal, she had to be lifted on to the commode, and after that back into her armchair. From the commode the lift was a two-person operation in order to dress her, and in those last months, as he was between jobs, that second person was usually my husband. She was not heavy for him, though her passivity gave no help in lifting, but he used to lift her quite roughly.

Then he realised how much he was rebelling against having to do this uncongenial task. As soon as he repented of his rebellion, and set his will to do it willingly, the whole way in which he lifted her changed. His inner attitude of obedience affected his outward handling. As he honoured her as a person, a parent, in his heart he was able physically to treat her better, and to honour her in practice.

SIMEON AND ANNA

Now there was a man in Jerusalem called Simeon, who was righteous and devout. He was waiting for the consolation of Israel, and the Holy Spirit was upon him. It had been revealed to him by the Holy Spirit that he would not die before he had seen the Lord's Christ. Moved by the Spirit, he went into the temple courts. When the parents brought in the child Jesus to do for him what the custom of the Law required, Simeon took him in his arms and praised God... The child's father and mother marvelled at what was said about him. Then Simeon blessed them... There was also a prophetess, Anna, the daughter of Phanuel, of the tribe of Asher. She was very old; she had lived with her husband seven years after her marriage, and then was a widow until she was eighty-four. She never left the temple but worshipped night and day, fasting and praying. Coming up to them at that very moment, she gave thanks to God and spoke about the child to all who were looking forward to the redemption of Jerusalem.

LUKE 2:25–28, 33–34, 36–38

'Grandmother isn't feeding herself properly,' the younger ones say, 'and she stays up half the night. It's draughty and uncomfortable in the temple, and she only has that dreadful old bed—can't we persuade her to live somewhere cosier?'

'Perhaps we should insist,' others suggest. 'She was married for such a short time, ages and ages ago, she can't still be mourning for her husband.'

'Is it 84 years since he died, or is she 84 years old?'

'No one can remember now. She is just very, very old, and she's so thin and frail. Perhaps it's our responsibility to take charge and make her move somewhere else.'

'But she's not gaga. She hasn't lost her marbles. If you talk to her she is right on the ball. I reckon she knows what she's doing. I reckon she has made a definite choice, even if she made it a long time ago. I reckon we should let her live as she wants to live.'

'Well, at least old Simeon keeps an eye on her. He's pretty ancient, but he must seem a mere boy to her.'

Waiting. Waiting on God, and waiting for the fulfilment of his promise. Not afraid of death but yearning for the promise to be fulfilled before death comes. Neither of them obviously productive. Each moving, not according to what other people think they should do but at the prompting of God's Spirit.

And so first Simeon, and then Anna, arrives at the precise time and place that God has designed, in order to prophesy—to speak God's words—over the baby Messiah, words for his parents to hear and begin to understand. Simeon and Anna were the culmination of the amazing events of Jesus' birth, not only because they lived close to God but also because their relatives had allowed them the freedom to be themselves, to live as they thought best.

A very high percentage of old people live alone. Although this may not initially have been their choice, they prefer it to the alternatives. We who care will watch the precarious way they fill the kettle, the slow, laborious movement, the hesitation on the stairs, the house gathering cobwebs in inaccessible places. We will be anxious for their safety, we children of a society obsessed with safety. We may want to take over and do it all for them.

But independence is part of dignity. For some people, all we can do is to be there, to affirm, to cherish, and to receive what is offered to us by shaking, wrinkled hands.

BEING OLD

AGEING

Remember also your Creator in the days of your youth, before the evil days come, and the years draw nigh, when you will say, 'I have no pleasure in them'; before the sun and the light and the moon and the stars are darkened and the clouds return after the rain; in the day when the keepers of the house tremble, and the strong men are bent, and the grinders cease because they are few, and those that look through the windows are dimmed, and the doors on the street are shut; when the sound of the grinding is low, and one rises up at the voice of a bird, and all the daughters of song are brought low; they are afraid also of what is high, and terrors are in the way; the almond tree blossoms, the grasshopper drags itself along and desire fails; because man goes to his eternal home, and the mourners go about the streets.

ECCLESIASTES 12:1–5

To state the obvious, one is not suddenly old. Old age comes gradually and, whatever the efforts to hold it at bay, be it colouring grey hair or any other device, inexorably we grow older. At what stage a person actually feels old is a complex combination of physical events, emotions and circumstances.

With our two then very small children I made a special visit home to celebrate my father's 80th birthday. When I arrived at the house he greeted me in gardening clothes, spry as could be. Yet earlier, just a year after I had married and abandoned him to less familiar secretarial help than mine, he was feeling very old and sad.

Later on again, when he was 82 or 83, he came to stay with us in Ripon in Yorkshire. He was becoming very lame and felt doddery. We had got to know a Canon of the cathedral who had befriended us, the young couple who risked bringing their two lively little boys in their bright red anoraks to worship every Sunday. Canon Bartlett was 93 and had a perpetual shake, yet on the occasions when he officiated at a service in the cathedral, life breathed through it. I invited him to coffee to meet my father, who said something about his age and feeling old. Canon Bartlett with a beaming smile exclaimed, 'My dear chap, you're a mere chicken!' Despite lameness and weariness, that put new life into my father.

Old age really hit him when he had an emergency prostate operation, without which he would have died painfully. Everything became slow and difficult, yet he was as definite as ever, with the same sense of humour. One day he decided he would like to walk the short distance to the village shop. He sat down for a while when we got there, and then we started back up the hill, at his slow two-stick pace. Reaching a seat about halfway, he subsided on to it gratefully, saying he could go no further, and I fetched the car. 'How ridiculous,' he said as we drove back round the corner. 'It's no distance at all!'

Physical limitations frustrated him, and he felt guilty that he did not have the will to do what he used to do, or even to do what still clearly cried out to be tackled. As my mother's arthritis worsened he would write to me, 'We're a couple of crocks.'

Maybe it's like this. Imagine an old woman is speaking.

Welcoming the young people as I would welcome any friend, I realised with a shock that they saw me as an old woman. That distanced me. I was something other, detached from them; somebody's grandmother, not a person in my own right. Yet I feel just the same. My white hair and wrinkled skin and hesitant walk have not altered the essential me.

Some of my tools are wearing out, that's all. Eyes and ears and joints. It's like trying to push an old lawnmower. The parts are worn and past repair, and the blades don't cut too well, so that pushing the mower is hard work. But I'm still there, doing the pushing—or having a rest.

Maybe my brain is one of the tools that is wearing out too. I don't always remember, and perhaps I get confused and do stupid things. But my soul, my essential mind, the real me, is still there. All the living I have done, all the loving, all the mistakes, all the joys, all that has gone to develop my character over the years, is none of it lost. It's only the tools that are letting me down.

I am not the tools. The tools are not me. Look beyond the tools, to the person I am. There is still a me to know.

A NEW LOVE

King David was now a very old man, and although his servants covered him with blankets, he could not keep warm. So his officials said to him, 'Your Majesty, let us find a young woman to stay with you and take care of you. She will lie close to you and keep you warm.' A search was made all over Israel for a beautiful girl, and in Shunem they found such a girl named Abishag, and brought her to the king. She was very beautiful, and waited on the king and took care of him, but he did not have intercourse with her.

1 KINGS 1:1–4 (GNB)

Sadie was a sociable, outgoing person who served in a shop well into retirement years. She lived alone after her husband died, and there came a time when it seemed wise for her to have some support. Her son Leslie arranged for her to have a room upstairs in his own house.

'It's for you,' he said, 'your own space with your own TV where you can do as you like. And with this little kitchen you can make your own snacks.'

He and his wife were out at work all day, so she was alone in 'her own space'. She came downstairs to join them for the evening meal, but she had the impression that she should not stay there afterwards but return upstairs. It was a lonely life.

Her daughter Jane was concerned that she was not making those snacks, that she was not feeding herself during the day. Her short-term memory began to wane, and she could not always remember whether or not she had eaten or when she had last seen Jane. Eventually Leslie and Jane found a retirement home for her and she moved in there.

She loved getting to know the other residents and, with regular meals, she put on weight and was altogether more healthy. Gilbert was a fellow resident. Despite the fact that he also had memory problems, they got on well together, looked out for each other. When they sat in the residents' lounge, they held hands.

Staff told Jane, 'This is upsetting the other residents. It will have to stop.' Leslie was afraid that if it continued Sadie would be forced to leave the retirement home. Jane, on the other hand, was adamant that their mother should have the freedom to form such a relationship, and she smiled when the pair said they would like to get married. She tackled the staff. What if other residents were embarrassed—or jealous? Just because Sadie was old and a bit confused, was this different from teenagers holding hands, going round the garden together?

Sadie's first thought on returning from an outing with Jane was for Gilbert, who would be keeping an eye out for her. They mattered to one another. One day they went out of the grounds for a walk and were found, quite lost, some distance away. After that they did have to be restrained from going out unaccompanied. But Jane won her point. They were allowed to carry on loving each other.

The intercourse side of sex is bound to fade with age, but

we still need relationships and physical contact. Modern society would be unlikely to countenance the solution that David's servants found to help keep him warm. But we may ask if we have the right to prevent an elderly couple from snuggling up together, enjoying a warmth they lost at widowhood. Would we be wrong to say 'dirty old man' if a present-day David took his charming carer into his bed, always provided the carer was willing? Should we not rather rejoice that old age need not deprive us of closeness?

LOSS

Lord, take us back to our land, just as the rain brings water back to dry riverbeds. Let those who wept as they sowed their seed, gather the harvest with joy!

PSALM 126:4–5 (GNB)

At the end of the book of Genesis, Jacob, making special arrangements for Rachel's grandsons before he himself died, said, 'For when I came from Paddan, Rachel to my sorrow died in the land of Canaan on the way, when there was still some distance to go to Ephrath; and I buried her on the way to Ephrath (that is, Bethlehem)' (Genesis 48:7, RSV).

Jacob was a nomad, travelling constantly on to where he could find pasture for his numerous flocks and herds. He had loved Rachel from the time he met her in her father's, his uncle's, house. His father-in-law had forced him to work for 14 years as bride price for Rachel, and even then it was many years before she had a child, Joseph. Then, when they were in transit, walking and riding their camels and donkeys, she went into labour with a precious second child.

Imagine his distress. He was responsible for a large family, huge flocks of sheep and herds of cattle and the servants that tended them, all on the move, and his beloved wife dies. He buries her, finds a nurse for the baby, erects a pillar of stones to mark her grave, and moves on, because he has to move on. There is no extended time of mourning, for pasture must be found.

As he grows older his life is bound up with the life of the lad Benjamin, the son of his old age, the son of Rachel, the son whose birth cost Rachel her life. His sons fear that if he were to lose Benjamin, he would die. So concerned are they that they are prepared at one time to stand hostage for Benjamin. The crisis passes; Jacob lives on, but always carrying the sorrow of his loss. The only reparation he can make is to the grandsons that Rachel never knew.

Reg, old and the last of his generation, was no stranger to loss. As a very young man he had seen a pal of his killed in the war. His mother, who had nurtured and encouraged him, had become dependent and pain-filled before she died. Yet both those losses were a long time ago. Now, one by one, his friends were keeling over. His brothers and sisters were all dead, even some of their children, and lastly his wife, companion of a lifetime, died too.

'He's coping very well with losing his wife,' people said. They noted how competently he fed himself, how neat and tidy he looked, how pleasant he was to the other old people in the Day Centre. 'Marvellous how he's coping,' they said.

And then his budgie died. He was devastated. He could talk of nothing else. The empty cage brought tears to his eyes whenever his glance fell on it. He would not hear of having another budgie. He seemed inconsolable. Now the pet bird who had chattered to him without requiring an answer, who had responded to him with head cocked and jewelled eye, who had depended undemandingly on him, was dead. In each of the other losses through his life he had 'coped'. The griefs had accumulated, unreleased. Perhaps this was one death too many, or maybe it was because it was of a different kind that it opened the floodgates of accumulated grief.

No one can reach old age without experiencing loss; not deaths only but redundancies, the failure of hopes and ambitions, the alienation of a child. There is the loss of initiative caused by failing powers, and the whole atmosphere of care where the chores are looked after and decisions are largely made by others. Loss is very much part of old age.

Perhaps the most traumatic loss, apart from the death of loved ones, is of a person's own home. For so long it has been the point of reference, the validation of identity. Each item of furniture tells a story and relates to family history.

When I was young I was impatient with my mother's attachment to the things in the house. Everything was precious, and a breakage resulted in major drama. Only in middle age did I begin to understand. She spent her childhood in a large and beautiful house. Each move as she grew up was not only linked to family loss and tragedy, it also meant that possessions had to be pared down to fit into more limited space. The family home that I knew was the fourth and smallest of the series. Therefore each thing in it had been kept because it held more significance than the things that had been parted with.

By the time she was 27, she was the only member of her immediate family left, so that for many years possessions constituted a major part of her security. Only as God healed her insecurities, and as my growth in understanding removed the threat of my impatience, could she release them.

Possessions form the framework of our lives. They are familiar friends, individually significant in a way that another person may find incomprehensible. Anyone liable to confusion will be more at peace and less confused if the few pieces of furniture that remain to them are arranged in roughly the same orientation in the new surroundings as they were originally. Just a small alleviation of the sense of loss.

Pray that the rain brings water back into their dry riverbeds…

NOT BEING A BURDEN

Barzillai the Gileadite also came down from Rogelim to cross the Jordan with the king and to send him on his way from there. Now Barzillai was a very old man, eighty years of age. He had provided for the king during his stay in Mahanaim, for he was a very wealthy man. The king said to Barzillai, 'Cross over with me and stay with me in Jerusalem, and I will provide for you.' But Barzillai answered the king, 'How many more years shall I live, that I should go up to Jerusalem with the king? I am now eighty years old. Can I tell the difference between what is good and what is not? Can your servant taste what he eats and drinks? Can I still hear the voices of men and women singers? Why should your servant be an added burden to my lord the king? Your servant will cross over the Jordan with the king for a short distance, but why should the king reward me in this way? Let your servant return, that I may die in my own town near the tomb of my father and mother.'

2 SAMUEL 19:31–37

King David had a son, Absalom, an exceptionally good-looking young man whom he had spoilt (2 Samuel 13—19). Over the years Absalom, with charm and cunning, had built up a following for himself, until suddenly David and his advisers realised that a coup was imminent and that they themselves were in grave danger. There was no time to lose. They left Jerusalem on foot, arranging things as they went, without any of the provisions a large body of men would need.

A short distance from Jerusalem, someone brought them donkeys to ride and some food and wine. Then they pressed on 30 or 40 miles to the River Jordan, dared not delay there, crossed it and went on up the tributary River Jabbok another 20 miles till, traumatised and exhausted, they reached Mahanaim.

There some wealthy locals, among them Barzillai, realising how tired and hungry and thirsty they must be after their desperate desert journey, brought them provisions. The grocery list was comprehensive: flour, various grains to be ground into flour as needed, honey, yoghurt, cheese, dry goods such as lentils, and even live sheep that could be slaughtered and prepared as the meat ration.

Groceries were not all that they contributed. They loaded up with bowls and mugs for eating and drinking, and they brought bedding for everyone.

David was enormously grateful, both on his own account and for his people who had so faithfully gone with him. He wanted to repay all this kindness in a tangible way. As he prepared to return across the Jordan, back towards Jerusalem, the opportunity arose, for Barzillai came down again from his home at Rogelim to set him on his way. It was then that David made him the offer of a pensioned place at court for the rest of his days.

Barzillai, however, was a realist. Arranging with his neighbours to provide for David at Mahanaim, he had thought through carefully all that they would need, making sure that the supply could be kept up throughout their exile in that place. Similarly he was a realist when David wanted to repay him for his kindness. He knew that David was offering him the luxuries of court life, delicate food, good wine, musical entertainment. He knew too that the limitations imposed on him by old age, evident deafness and the loss of a sense of taste, would prevent him enjoying any of it. His preference was to be allowed to carry on where he belonged and to die in his own setting.

Also, he did not want to be a burden to his lord the king. Not to be a burden to the younger generation—that is a wish many people express. Somehow it is more acceptable to be cared for by paid staff, if need be, than by the children one has reared. That those children, whom parents have nurtured and encouraged and then released to lead their own lives, that they should become the nurturers is hard to stomach. It is a role reversal which reverses more than function. And we cannot pretend that such care may not be a burden.

There are a couple of puzzling verses about burdens in Galatians 6:2, 5. To start with, Paul says, 'Carry each other's burdens, and in this way you will fulfil the law of Christ.' As the law of Christ is the law of love, this makes sense, helping each other with each other's burdens. But then a couple of verses later he says, 'Each one should carry his own load.'

Thinking about this, and assuming that Paul is not contradicting himself, it seems to me that what it is saying is, 'Help each other out, but don't offload your legitimate responsibilities on to other people.' There are ways and ways of being a burden!

Jesus said, 'Come to me, all you who are weary and burdened, and I will give you rest. Take my yoke upon you and learn from me, for I am gentle and humble in heart, and you will find rest for your souls. For my yoke is easy and my burden is light' (Matthew 11:28–30).

I once rode on an ox cart in Nepal. The cart was pulled by two oxen, their necks side by side under the wooden yoke. The one on the left got hardly any attention from the carter, but the one on the right needed frequent correction. The carter explained that the one on the right was a youngster and that the real training was being given by the older ox which was sharing the yoke with him. He plodded patiently on, putting up with the youngster's fits and starts and wandering off course, teaching him the job while taking at least half the load.

Both older and younger among us could look on this whole burden business as a stage in God's training.

WHERE TO CARE

Abraham took another wife, whose name was Keturah... Altogether, Abraham lived a hundred and seventy-five years. Then Abraham breathed his last and died at a good old age.

GENESIS 25:1, 7–8

Jacob came home to his father Isaac in Mamre... where Abraham and Isaac had stayed. Isaac lived a hundred and eighty years. Then he breathed his last and died and was gathered to his people, old and full of years. And his sons Esau and Jacob buried him.

GENESIS 35:27–29 (ABRIDGED)

Pharaoh said to Joseph, 'Your father and your brothers have come to you, and the land of Egypt is before you; settle your father and your brothers in the best part of the land. Let them live in Goshen...' So Joseph settled his father and his brothers in Egypt and gave them property in the best part of the land, the district of Rameses, as Pharaoh directed. Joseph also provided his father and his brothers and all his father's household with food, according to the number of their children.

GENESIS 47:5–6, 11–12

Yet again Genesis illustrates what is relevant and emotive to us today, this time regarding the options of where to care.

My father-in-law's old age reminds me of Abraham. Widowed, he married a lifelong family friend ten years his junior and they spent a contented 20 years together, sharing interests and welcoming each other's children and grandchildren. At the very end of his life his wife needed some paid nursing help and we were able to give her an occasional 'day off' or holiday away, but he remained at home until he died 'full of years' at 91.

Not much is recorded of Isaac's old age, but a certain amount can be pieced together. For years he and his household had been nomadic, always moving on to find water and pasture until the digging and securing of two wells right down in the south of the land of Canaan settled them around Beersheba. Isaac was blind for the last 20 or 30 years of his life, which may have been another reason for him taking to a more static lifestyle. He made just one major move. Twenty years or more after he first expected to die, he moved his household to the place where his parents were buried, ever ready for his own death.

Looking at Isaac's declining years, we hear of no immediate family with him. His favourite son Esau was away the other side of the rift valley, and Jacob was even further away in Haran, near the Upper Euphrates, until his slow move back to Canaan. While in practical terms each son needed space to support his flocks and cattle, in emotional terms both may well have withdrawn to be out of reach of parental manipulation. There had been such a pattern of manipulation, by Isaac, by Rebekah, by Jacob, with Esau plodding along trying to please everyone.

Isaac's household would have consisted of servants and their families working together to look after him, not unlike a retirement or nursing home. It probably worked well for him, a solitary man by nature, and Jacob did make it back to see him before he died.

These arrangements 'happened' but it is not always that simple for us, with complex financial concerns and an apparently wide range of options. We're not just dealing with arrangements, either. We are looking at an interlacing of individuals, each of whom has a definite will of their own and often a strong attachment to their own place. Discussion, decisions and moves are the more difficult in a family where one or more members have a habit of domination or manipulation.

I did hear about an old man who had steadily blackmailed his family's emotions for years, seemingly entirely self-centred. He reached a point when he had to have care. None of his family could face living with him, yet they felt terribly guilty when they arranged for him to move into a retirement home. They expected the worst, but in fact his new environment seemed to have a positive effect on his attitude. Visiting him after he had settled in, they found that he was being friendly and generous to his fellow residents and was even ready to be interested in his family's doings.

Households that once employed a nanny often looked on her as part of their family and kept in close touch even after she had moved away to other positions. Alison was concerned for the family nanny who, after a lifetime of caring for children, had reached the stage of needing care herself. She agonised over whether she should take her into her own home to look after her, but with some trepidation eventually found her a place in a Salvation Army retirement home.

It was the right decision, and Nanny was transformed. She enjoyed the other residents' company and the love and care in a disciplined framework. Old age had made everything an effort, tempting her to let things slip, but the ordered day in the home restored to her a setting as familiar as the 'well-ordered nurseries' which she had run in former times. Best of all, she discovered Jesus for herself and became a Christian.

Nothing could have been more different from moving into a retirement home than Jacob's final house move. Although Joseph, at Pharaoh's command, sent carts to fetch him and all his family from the land of Canaan, it was a risky business to travel nearly 300 miles through a drought-ridden wilderness with all their flocks and herds. Old people do have to be allowed to take risks if they want to. We've only one life to live and it is more fun to take the odd risk than to prolong an existence wrapped in cotton wool.

Jacob's family virtually emigrated, and he undoubtedly spent his last years surrounded by children, grandchildren and probably great-grandchildren. For all the anxiety and distress they had caused him in the past, he must have been relieved to be settled with them in comfortable, prosperous surroundings under the protection of his dear son Joseph. It sounds pretty good to me.

RETELLING THE STORY

In the future, when your son asks you, 'What is the meaning of the stipulations, decrees and laws the Lord our God has commanded you?' tell him: 'We were slaves of Pharaoh in Egypt, but the Lord brought us out of Egypt with a mighty hand. Before our eyes the Lord sent miraculous signs and wonders—great and terrible—upon Egypt and Pharaoh and his whole household. But he brought us out from there to bring us in and give us the land that he promised on oath to our forefathers. The Lord commanded us to obey all these decrees and to fear the Lord our God, so that we might always prosper and be kept alive, as is the case today.'

DEUTERONOMY 6:20–24

Telling our story, and hearing the story of the people from whom we are sprung, is of enormous importance, both for the teller and for the hearers. Without a sense of history our view of the present and of ourselves is limited and handicapped. The telling and the hearing bring healing and growth.

I have known Marion and Graham for many years and on one of my visits to them I heard their story of caring. It was quite different from my own, unique as anyone's own story will be, yet with universal resonances.

When Graham's mother began to need care, he and

Marion neither moved in with her, which would have been impractical, nor did they have her to live with them. They did suggest it. Mother was horrified. 'Then I really would be lonely,' she said, and they realised that she was right. Theirs was a busy household with everyone, adults and their children, in and out and mostly out, and in their home she would have been detached from many of her existing contacts, alone and lonely. She was a sociable person and needed people around her. She also wanted to determine herself how she would lead her own life.

So she used her slender income to live in a retirement home, or more accurately a series of retirement homes, where she charmed the domestic staff but often came into conflict with her fellow residents, whom she somehow regarded as rivals. She was one of those people for whom a new place was perfect until some upset totally changed her mind and then she insisted on moving elsewhere.

After a while, as her abilities decreased and her weight increased, she needed actual nursing, and Marion spent many hours investigating nursing homes, arranging moves when required, visiting regularly and mollifying both mother-in-law and staff. Higher fees meant that Graham had to contribute, and this continued through a good many years since his mother lived to be over 90.

Graham was self-employed, and time spent visiting meant time lost for work, and if work were lost he could not pay the nursing home. Yet the highest cost to Graham was emotional. His mother had always been dramatic. From childhood Graham had been uncomfortable about her dramas, and never certain how much of what she said was fact and how much she had embroidered. He had been raised largely by her parents and when he was back with her he had found that he did not really like her. Now, in that costly process of spending time with her, he learnt deeply about her and about himself.

As he sat by his mother, she talked in detail of her early life. This was not idle rambling but specific topics. It was as if she were completely back in the situation she described, and indeed her behaviour was often that of a teenager, irresponsible, unpredictable and mischievous.

She must have gone over the incidents in her life many times, crafting them to how she believed they should be or how she was convinced they had occurred. Any story she told for a second or third time would be in precisely the same words and terms as the first, so indelibly were they imprinted on her memory. She would talk for about 20 minutes, as if totally in a specific and remote time of her life, until the topic was exhausted. Then she would fall asleep, and when she next awoke she would be in another entirely different time and circumstance.

She was not directly telling her son these things. Often it was as if she were addressing her father—'It's no good pretending, I know perfectly well that this is how it was with Uncle Wilfred'—family matters, scandals and black sheep that Graham had vaguely suspected and was enthralled to be told. With no one at all now to 'tut tut' her, she cheerfully revealed the events, the gossip, the dramas, that had made up her life.

One can only guess at what this retelling was doing for her. Maybe it resolved the taboos imposed on her by family or social convention. Maybe it allowed her to settle old scores and to forgive. Maybe it helped to heal old hurts.

Graham was not just collecting interesting family information, he was getting to know his mother in a new way. As he came to know and understand, he could more readily accept and forgive her, all of which adds up to love. This distressing period was a growing and character-forming time for him.

'I'm so glad,' she said towards the end, 'that we've had this time together.'

FAMILY STRESS

JACOB AND SONS

Israel said to Joseph, 'As you know, your brothers are grazing the flocks near Shechem... Go and see if all is well with your brothers and with the flocks, and bring word back to me.' ... So Joseph went after his brothers and found them near Dothan. But they saw him in the distance, and before he reached them, they plotted to kill him. 'Here comes that dreamer!' they said to each other. 'Come now, let's kill him and throw him into one of these cisterns and say that a ferocious animal devoured him. Then we'll see what comes of his dreams.'

GENESIS 37:13–14, 17–20 (ABRIDGED)

It can be so discouraging to read about splendid Christian families who seem to have it all together, while we know that in many ways we have not. Yet here is a family which had been specially chosen by God, promised blessings not only to themselves but through them to all peoples, and they are at sixes and sevens.

The ten brothers were jealous, and not only of young Joseph's 'amazing technicolor dreamcoat' and their father's favouritism towards him. He was only 17 when, having been shepherding the flock of sheep with some of his half-brothers, he had split on them to Jacob about their ill conduct.

They hated him for that, but worse was to come. Joseph

had a couple of dreams which he was rash enough to tell them. In the first one they were together in a field, binding sheaves of corn, when his sheaf stood upright and all the eleven others gathered round and bowed down to it.

'Ha!' they said. 'Cocky youngster! Do you suppose you're going to reign over us?'

Then he had a second dream which implied that not only his brothers but the sun and the moon (their parents?) as well would be bowing down to him. This was intolerable. No doubt the brothers were talking about it all while dear Joseph was at home with Dad, and fed each other's jealousy and hatred. And now, suspecting perhaps that Joseph had been sent to report back on them, they hatched their plot.

Reuben, the eldest of the brothers, did not openly oppose them but tried to divert their plan so that perhaps he could rescue Joseph later on. He persuaded them to throw him into an empty cistern out there in the desert, rather than kill him. When Joseph arrived they did just that. They stripped him of his special coat and threw him into a nearby cistern, a water reservoir carved out of the rock, which mercifully had no water in it. Then they sat down and ate their picnic lunch.

They were not far from a trade route and soon they spotted a caravan of merchants with camels loaded with spices, coming along towards them. Judah had a bright idea. Killing Joseph was not a particularly profitable thing to do; why not sell him to these traders, who would take him on their way and put him up for sale in Egypt? Profit all round and goodbye to Joseph. In the later Jewish law, to sell someone into slavery against their will was considered a grave crime, and this was probably so even at this era, yet Judah's brothers agreed with him and they did as he suggested. They sold Joseph to the Midianite traders.

Reuben had evidently wandered off before the deed was done, and he was tremendously distressed on rejoining them to discover that Joseph was gone. But he did not try to stop his brothers killing a goat, dipping the beautiful robe in its blood, and reporting to their father that Joseph must have been killed—torn to pieces and devoured—by a wild animal. He went along with the deception and, the ultimate deceit, joined with them in trying to comfort their father in his grief and distress. Lies compounded calumny and lies.

There were other incidents too, which could have shocked the readers of the most sensational tabloid.

ONLY DAUGHTER RAPED!

Brothers take terrible vengeance—
Shechem a slaughter house

Every man killed, women and children abducted

This is how the headlines could have run, and surely the authorities would have been hot on the trail.

Not long after the Shechem incident, the tabloids had another scoop about the goings-on of this family:

INCEST!

Eldest son of respected cattle-rancher
has sex with father's concubine

Father refuses to comment

That was not all. Judah got into a highly improper mess with his own daughter-in-law which could have kept the gossip columns going for months. Like many fathers today, Jacob seemed able to do nothing more than protest.

So whatever skeletons there are in your family cupboard, take heart. God has been there before and he has a way out.

LIVING STONES

Rid yourselves of all malice and all deceit, hypocrisy, envy, and slander of every kind. Like newborn babies, crave pure spiritual milk, so that by it you may grow up in your salvation, now that you have tasted that the Lord is good. As you come to him, the living Stone—rejected by men but chosen by God and precious to him—you also, like living stones, are being built into a spiritual house.

1 PETER 2:1–5

At a craft fair I stood enthralled at the stand where someone who made jewellery was demonstrating how stones are polished. The raw stones were coloured but quite dull. Alongside them he showed others in a polishing machine that gently rocked them in a mixture of fine grit and water. The process, he told me, lasted months. Back and forth the stones would go, knocking against each other, ground by the grit, the small knocks and irritations, for week after week. And at the end they emerged shiny and brilliant.

This could be a picture of how God shapes us up through the frictions of living together, of caring for a failing old parent.

But, we may ask, what is he shaping us up for? What is the ultimate objective? Most of us must at one time or another have wondered why we are here, what purpose our lives have. Some of the stock answers do not sound particularly compelling. Perpetuating my species, for instance, does not grab me as a reason for living. Making the world a better place for the next generation is a bit beyond me, and mostly mankind seems intent on making it a worse place.

To hear that God created us to be his friends and companions can be mind-boggling, yet this alone gives real meaning and purpose to living. We have made a mess of his initial creation. We have abused the free will he gave us, preferring our own will to his, and we do not even try to live the way he intended. But even so he loves us, each one individually, and offers us the means of becoming people who can enjoy companionship with him.

The more you get to know someone special who loves you dearly, the more you love them and the more you want to be with them. From the first 'step in the dark' of trusting God as he showed himself in Jesus, the response of love is to want to learn more of this loving Father, and of how he wants us to be. He on his side offers us training to be people who can delight in eternal life with him, a training that can at times be painful.

Even Jesus, in his humanity, had to endure painful training, and if we are Jesus' brothers and sisters through being reborn into God's family, we can expect the same sort of training and discipline that he was given, and the same acceptance, love and, yes, even joy, as we allow it to happen.

In 1 Peter 2:5, Peter compares us to a different sort of stone—not the kind used by a jeweller but a construction stone for building the temple of which Christ is the cornerstone. I have often found that the Bible is its own best expositor, that in exploring its books we can come across things that relate to other parts and help us to understand them. This happened to me about stones.

I was reading one day in 1 Kings 6 about the building of Solomon's temple, and I was fascinated by all the detailed specifications and, in particular, by all it said about the stones that were used. I delved into our encyclopedia to find out about stone-masonry, and began to realise just how special those stones were.

Most stones for building are dressed only on the side that will face outwards. But the stones for the temple were to be dressed on both sides, and this despite the fact that on the inside the walls were to be completely covered with cedar-wood panelling. Normally stones are made only roughly level on top and underneath, relying on a thin layer of mortar to bond them together. But the temple stones had their tops and bottoms dressed perfectly flat and level, giving such an exact fit when they were built together that, still today, it is impossible to get a knife blade between those stones that remain.

All this shaping had to be done at the quarry from which they had been cut, so that there was no noise at the temple building site. And after all the shaping had been completed, they were left at the quarry for up to three years, to weather. Weathering dried out the 'sap' in them, hardened them up, and made them lighter to transport.

It suddenly struck me that these are the stones to which Peter likens us in his letter, living stones building the temple—or kingdom—of God. I thought how often I have been to church rough-hewn, somehow expecting God to shape me up in the course of worship. And what a hurry I have been in, looking for instant holiness, instant usefulness, rapid rapport with God! I also thought of the times he has dealt with me, sometimes drastically, in the quarry of family life.

LOAD-BEARING

Christ in you, the hope of glory.

COLOSSIANS 1:27

The God who said, 'Out of darkness the light shall shine!' is the same God who made his light shine in our hearts, to bring us the light of the knowledge of God's glory shining in the face of Christ. Yet we who have this spiritual treasure are like common clay pots, in order to show that the supreme power belongs to God, not to us. We are often troubled, but not crushed; sometimes in doubt, but never in despair; there are many enemies, but we are never without a friend; and though badly hurt at times, we are not destroyed. At all times we carry in our mortal bodies the death of Jesus, so that his life also may be seen in our bodies.

2 CORINTHIANS 4:6–10 (GNB)

My husband is a civil engineer by training, and I asked him about reinforced concrete beams, for it occurred to me that there is a parallel with a Christian family and how it reacts to the stress of caring for an elderly relative.

Concrete by itself cannot carry any great weight, because if it bends it cracks. To give it strength and elasticity it needs steel inside it. The very strongest beams are those that are 'pre-stressed', which means that the steel has taken up the stress before being encased in the concrete.

But it is not just a matter of being encased. The bond or grip between the steel and the concrete is vital to the strength of the beam. First of all the steel must be clean, with no foreign substance between steel and concrete. The concrete itself needs to be of a good consistent mixture. The bond, an intimate relationship, is formed chemically as the concrete cures around the steel.

If the concrete is of a consistent quality, it will 'fail' where the effect of the load produces greatest stress. The technical word 'fail' does not mean that the beam collapses, but that cracks appear in the concrete. It is hardly surprising that if the beam is overloaded, cracks will appear at the point of that overload.

If, however, the quality of the concrete is not consistent, so that some parts of the beam contain concrete of a stronger mixture than others, then less than the maximum load for which it was designed may cause failure at unexpected points. In the general area of greatest stress, 'failure' in the form of cracks will show up wherever there are slight weaknesses.

This could be a picture of the family that has Jesus at its centre. The steel of the Spirit gives it strength and elasticity and has indeed already taken the stress. The strength of the family depends on how closely bonded it has become with Jesus, a 'chemical cure' that mercifully is more of an ongoing process than that of concrete. Heavy loads on the family will cause cracks to appear, but very often those cracks will indicate where there were already weaknesses. The load has caused the appearance of the weaknesses; it has not caused the weaknesses themselves.

The Spirit enables us to carry the load, and he also allows

us to look honestly at the cracks and maybe to repair them. Sometimes, sadly, the cracks that were there before the load was applied are not repairable and a piece of the concrete falls off. One friend of mine moved with her children into her widowed father's home to care for him, expecting that when military duties allowed, her husband would join them. She waited and waited, but in the end he opted to make the separation permanent, and they were divorced. It could not be said that the choice to look after her father had caused the split, but the load that that caring had imposed revealed an existing flaw in their marriage and worsened it.

It would be nonsense to suggest that caring for the very old is not a load, but it could be wrong necessarily to blame the load for cracks and failures. The family may be unwilling to give. The solitary carer who breaks down may always have found difficulty in receiving help. Or the weaknesses may be at an emotional level. For some of us the umbilical cord has never been severed other than physically. We may have 'left father and mother and cleaved to wife (or husband, or career)' in that we have left home and live elsewhere, but may remain in the dependent child relationship inside ourselves. The children of dominant parents have this problem in acute form.

Another weak point may be that the family has never much communicated within itself. As a result the members know very little about each other and how the other members of the family tick. The younger generation may know little about their parents' past life, and even less about their grandparents, so that if three generations are brought under one roof there is no common history to foster understanding.

The amazing thing about the reinforced concrete beam is that even when the beam has 'failed', with huge deflection, lumps of concrete broken off and cracks obvious and open, it will continue to carry load because of the steel reinforcing within it.

Load-bearing but cracking up! Hanging on to God but falling apart as people! Is that really such an encouraging picture?

You can patch up the cracks, of course. You can put in fresh concrete and make it all look better—a cosmetic job. Circumstances change, and we put a brave face on things, giving the world the impression that we and our family are OK. 'We're fine,' we say. A good cosmetic job. But the cracks and the weaknesses that caused them are only hidden. They are still there, under the repairs.

There are choices. We can back off entirely. We can allow conflicts to continue and become embedded in our family life. Or we can allow God to change us, to recreate the concrete around his steel reinforcement, replacing the defective concrete with new, top-quality stuff through the interplay of family members.

A WISE FATHER-IN-LAW

Now Jethro, the priest of Midian and father-in-law of Moses, heard of everything God had done for Moses and for his people Israel, and how the Lord had brought Israel out of Egypt. Jethro... came to him in the desert, where he was camped near the mountain of God... Moses went out to meet [him] and bowed down and kissed him...

The next day Moses took his seat to serve as judge for the people, and they stood around him from morning till evening. When his father-in-law saw all that Moses was doing for the people, he said, 'What is this you are doing for the people? Why do you alone sit as judge, while all these people stand round you from morning till evening?' Moses answered him, 'Because the people come to me to seek God's will. Whenever they have a dispute, it is brought to me, and I decide between the parties and inform them of God's decrees and laws.' Moses' father-in-law replied, 'What you are doing is not good. You and these people who come to you will only wear yourselves out. The work is too heavy for you; you cannot handle it alone. Listen now to me and I will give you some advice, and may God be with you... Select capable men from all the people—men who fear God, trustworthy men who hate dishonest gain—and appoint them as officials over thousands, hundreds, fifties and tens... That will make your load lighter, because they will share it with you...' Moses listened to his father-in-law and did everything he said.

EXODUS 18:1–24 (ABRIDGED)

None of my family were keen to live with Gran. They did not much like her and her sharp tongue. The first summer holidays that we spent in her house were possible because of lots of outside activities and because we perceived the arrangement as temporary. But it turned out not to be temporary, until for the last year of her life her home was our home, and we were truly in it together.

I'm sure one thing God wanted to teach us was that none of us can fulfil all roles. We need to operate as a body.

Watching my elder son showing Gran his drawings and including her in what he was doing, I felt guilty because that sort of shared interest was really difficult for me. The practical side of caring I could manage, even the dirty and unpleasant bits, and I could keep the household running, clean and fed. I disliked myself for being unable or unwilling to do what he was doing.

Then there was the friend who on some mornings helped to get my mother up. After breakfast she would look at pictures with her and notice the smallest hint of communication. Why could I not do that too? Other friends who were teachers could pick up words where I heard only gibberish.

I felt guilty about this, until I began to see that each member of the family had particular gifts and I must rejoice in those. I could rejoice that the gaps in my own care for my mother could be made up by others, family or friends.

A lack that I had no difficulty in admitting was a lack of physical strength. We were fortunate in being able to have help from a local Family Support Unit, which several days a week provided a stalwart lady to help lift my mother out of bed in the morning and wash and dress her. There were other friends too, even the man who looked after her garden, who came to my rescue when lifting was required.

One Christmas we invited members of two families to a sort of party. Our daughter's friend Samantha had lost her voice with laryngitis. Unable to speak, she sat silently the whole evening on a stool at Gran's feet, giving wordless but real companionship. No one could doubt that my mother was appreciating this, a youngster just being with her, undemanding.

Our elder son, sitting beside his grandmother when he was drawing, allowed her to enter into the art which had been such an important part of her life. He would look at photo albums and picture books with her. As her ability to speak deteriorated, there were no more sharp remarks to contend with, just her warm smile. Our second son was a great asset at meals, helping and restraining her, while our daughter just loved her, and my husband was a constant support for me.

Each person was making an individual and sometimes costly contribution, learning to relate to Gran and at the same time learning to relate to one another.

ACCEPTANCE

Let us give thanks to the God and Father of our Lord Jesus Christ! For in our union with Christ he has blessed us by giving us every spiritual blessing in the heavenly world. Even before the world was made, God had already chosen us to be his through our union with Christ, so that we would be holy and without fault before him. Because of his love God had already decided that through Jesus Christ he would make us his sons—this was his pleasure and purpose. Let us praise God for his glorious grace, for the free gift he gave us in his dear Son! [KJV: To the praise of the glory of his grace, wherein he hath made us accepted in the beloved.] For by the death of Christ we are set free, that is, our sins are forgiven. How great is the grace of God which he gave to us in such large measure!

EPHESIANS 1:3–8 (GNB)

Both children and aged relatives can embarrass us with their frank and penetrating questions or comments that ignore polite conventions. Are we bothered because we are afraid that other people will be bothered, or because we feel that such outspokenness shows us up? Or do we fear that such remarks somehow demean the person making them? Other people can wonderfully resolve such embarrassment, and God himself can enable us to receive their help.

One of the two most significant instances of healing that I have received concerned the feeling of not being wanted.

The trigger was an exercise class. In the half-time break I said to someone I particularly liked, 'Come and have lunch. I've made an enormous pot of soup.'

'Sorry,' she said, 'I'm going to lunch with Gill.'

To my astonishment, I was devastated. Back home I was desperate to understand my own reaction, to get to the bottom of it and sort it out, but I had to wait four whole days before my regular weekly meeting with two friends to pray. Those days seemed endless. Somehow I could not sort this out on my own, I needed them to wait on God and release his Spirit in and for me. In the event, that was indeed their role—they did not do anything.

I told them what had happened. As we silently sought God, I began to cry, and the crying sounded like a baby's. I recalled my mother telling me how, after my very difficult birth, I was wrapped up and put aside while staff attended to her urgent needs. Suddenly, she had told me, the nurse thrust me into her arms saying, 'Quick, give her a kiss!' for they thought that I would die. 'Oh!' my mother said. 'She's so cold!'

With my inner eye I 'saw' that baby put aside, and she (I) said, 'They don't want me.' And then in the inexplicable way that God does, he put the assurance right into my heart that I am wanted; I am acceptable. Not only did I know then in my head that I had been a much-wanted daughter, I knew it for a surety in my inmost being also.

A seal was put to this assurance on a later occasion, praying with people who were staying next door, whom I did not know well but who wanted to have a time of prayer together. For some reason I told them how, when teams were picked at school, I was always left to the last. I always had the feeling that they were thinking, 'Oh bad luck, you'll have to have Alexine' (overgrown and clumsy with no eye for a ball as I was). God gave Michael a word which made all the difference: 'Before the foundation of the world, God picked you for his team.' Amazing!

That healing opened my heart to friends' reassurances which previously I would not have believed. For instance, as senile dementia advanced, my mother would make a very loud noise. It had begun as 'O dear, O dear,' then reduced to 'Oh, Oh,' and finally became a roar of amazing volume. It might denote discomfort, or boredom, or 'It's time you noticed me,' or maybe it was just a comment on the moment. Members of our church congregation assured me that it did not worry them during the services, and those who had long known her spoke of her with such warm affection that I too learnt to accept it and not to be embarrassed. They were not unaware of some of her faults and foibles, but they accepted her as herself.

Acceptance helps one to be accepting. When I first looked after my mother and she was at the stage of making unexpected and inconsequential remarks, I was tensely on the defensive if friends visited us. Sometimes she seemed afraid that they might be staying the night, and would demand to know where they had put their suitcase, and hadn't I better phone the local hotel for a room for them. Young men, friends of our sons, would be told, 'You need a haircut.' If any visitor stayed longer than she wanted, she would say, 'Goodbye, it's time you were going,' and only sometimes could I smile.

Early on in our caring, my brother had written to me, '"Just as I am"; in acceptance lies the opportunity for change. How important that we should make her climate a warm, accepting, valuing one so that there can be the possibility of freedom.'

And as the Lord changed me and I learnt to accept her, the whole embarrassment thing simmered down.

Later on, a visiting friend said how normal and natural our meal had seemed. By that time, I was feeding my mother with a spoon, and we had to have a 'no-go area' on the table as far as she could reach; otherwise she would suddenly grab things, drop a napkin ring into her water or cover her food with salt. My own plate would be just beyond the no-go area, and I could give my attention to her, feeding both her and myself, and chatting to the others without bother and without embarrassment.

WHAT ABOUT ME?

TO CARE OR NOT TO CARE

Show me, O Lord, my life's end and the number of my days; let me know how fleeting is my life. You have made my days a mere handbreadth; the span of my years is as nothing before you. Each man's life is but a breath. Man is a mere phantom as he goes to and fro: he bustles about, but only in vain; he heaps up wealth, not knowing who will get it. But now, Lord, what do I look for? My hope is in you.

PSALM 39:4–7

My days are swifter than a runner; they fly away without a glimpse of joy. They skim past like boats of papyrus, like eagles swooping down on their prey.

JOB 9:25–26

How frail is man, how few his days, how full of trouble! He blossoms for a moment like a flower—and withers; as the shadow of a passing cloud, he quickly disappears.

JOB 14:1–2 (LB)

A depressing lot of verses, I always thought. There are others of the same ilk, about us being like grass that comes up one day and is dry and ready to be disposed of the next. I assumed that they were written by elderly (or, in Job's case, afflicted) people who did not expect to live much longer and who felt that their life had been all too short and fruitless. Time seems to go faster and faster the older one grows, and it must have something to do with that.

But what excites me about the Bible is the way the Holy Spirit can give a completely new slant on a familiar passage, teaching something that one previously had no idea it contained. I've watched cloud shadows race across the landscape, and maybe it was that image that caught my attention. I began to see that all these verses are not just for the ancient and disappointed, but that in a way they apply to me, now.

Our friend Roy did his pastoral training in two different churches under two very different ministers. For the first of the two, a great evangelist, the work was everything. He achieved a great deal during his incumbency. The Holy Spirit moved powerfully within the church, which grew and flourished. But then he moved on, and things fell apart. There were lots of reasons why this happened, not least, no doubt, that the enemy of salvation, the Devil, was ready to take any chance that came his way to destroy what had been built. But one cause was that the very ordinary church members had not been trained in administration and leadership.

For the second minister, training people was top priority, and Roy told me with some anguish that everything, every meeting, took absolutely ages. Less work was got through, yet unlikely people were being eased into taking responsibility for church life and built up for the future.

These were Roy's comments, not his judgment, and I would not presume to criticise either of his ministers on such limited information, but what he told me made me take quite a hard look at myself.

As someone who is good at getting things done, I realise how easily things, jobs, can come before people. When my children were little, it struck me how often I was annoyed with them because of possible damage to some piece of furniture, or because they had interrupted what I was doing.

Later on, rushing to get supper at the end of a hectic day, I would refuse to break off for the few seconds needed to inspect the model one of the children had been painstakingly working on all afternoon and wanted to show me. Admiring it later on did not amend the dismissiveness of that vital moment. The child's crestfallen face rebuked me again and again. The 'flower' opens, blooms, fades so quickly, and the chance to appreciate, to affirm, is so fleeting, yet it is of great significance in building relationships, the stuff of which eternal life is made.

It's not that the work, the job, is necessarily unimportant. It is a matter of priorities. Anyone who is in work these days seems to be under enormous pressure with deadlines, yet sometimes it may be worth pausing and asking, 'Is this going to skim past, like boats of papyrus, or like the shadow of a passing cloud?' And when it comes to choosing whether or not to help care for an elderly relative, maybe it is time for some deep heart-searching.

We need to ask questions like, is my job or career my way of telling myself that I am worthwhile—and might God have a better way of doing that for me? What are my motives for seeking promotion, for retaining a place in the career structure? Is my income required for actual needs, or for things that I and my family could do without?

My friend Jane was a high-powered and highly paid marketing executive. Year after year she won awards for her successes. Each award was marked by a medal, or 'gong', as they all called it. She had quite a collection.

Jane had long been a Christian but there came a point when she experienced a new filling by the Holy Spirit and began to hear God in a new way. From time to time she would realise that this or that aspect of her life was not pleasing to him and that he was asking her to cut it out. She tried to obey each time.

The gongs issue came as a big challenge. The gongs had been such a reassurance to her of her value, such a boost to her self-esteem, but God said that they did not mean very much to him. He wanted her confidence to be in him and not in marketing awards. Where was her identity?

She struggled and she prayed, and in the end she gathered them all up and drove to the household disposal dump. One by one she threw the bin bags containing the medals into a skip, and as the last one clattered down inside, she experienced God's Holy Spirit tangibly upon her. She found herself lying in the rubbish, praying and praising in tongues to the amazement and concern of the people around. From then on, God gave her a new focus, a new perspective, a new calling to serve his people in a new way.

Jane told me, 'I felt the Holy Spirit say that these things were no longer my accreditation, that he would now be my accreditation.'

GREATER LOVE...

As the Father has loved me, so have I loved you. Now remain in my love. If you obey my commands, you will remain in my love, just as I have obeyed my Father's commands and remain in his love. I have told you this so that my joy may be in you and that your joy may be complete. My command is this: Love each other as I have loved you. Greater love has no one than this, that he lay down his life for his friends. You are my friends if you do what I command.

JOHN 15:9–14

I had always thought that—apart from Jesus himself—laying down one's life applied to martyrs and heroes. It meant that in the unlikely event of my friend's life being threatened, I ought to be prepared, if I really love my friend, to be killed in his place—a remote possibility; so remote that I need hardly consider it.

But thinking about this, I began to see connections with other things that Jesus said. He said, 'If anyone would come after me, he must deny himself and take up his cross and follow me. For whoever wants to save his life will lose it, but whoever loses his life for me and for the gospel will save it' (Mark 8:34–35). Count the cost, he said (in Luke's parallel passage), for 'any of you who does not give up everything he has cannot be my disciple' (Luke 14:33).

So does that mean that I must give away to the poor everything I have, like the rich young ruler? Is that the only way to be Jesus' disciple? Ah! but perhaps there is a let-out! In the first few verses of Luke 8, we read about the women who provided for Jesus and his disciples out of their own means. If they had given everything away to the poor, they would not have had any means with which to support Jesus. So it looks as if the instruction to part with all possessions may be only for some people, and not the universal condition of discipleship.

But Jesus did say 'anyone', and that suggests that it must be meant for everyone. In that case, might there be a deeper meaning to denying ourselves and giving up all that we have? Might it be something to do with attitude?

My understanding began to dawn in the middle of one night. My mother had woken me. As I urged her on to the commode beside her bed, my remarks and instructions were surly. Then, as I knelt to ease her into fresh pyjamas, she said, 'Don't sound so cross!'

There had been many occasions in the past when she had said (with justification), 'Don't sound so cross.' But this time it stopped me in my tracks and made me think. Why was I speaking crossly? Did it help the situation? What in fact was there to be cross about? As I faced up to this crossness of mine, it dawned on me that the root of it was self-pity.

I was sorry for myself at having been woken in the night. I was sorry for myself at having to get up and try to alleviate my mother's sleeplessness. I was sorry for myself doing all the mopping-up when I would rather be in bed, and I was taking it all out on her.

I never wanted to be a geriatric nurse. All my plans for the next few years had evaporated while I settled into the lonely, demanding half-life of caring for a frail, elderly, confused parent. Maybe I had cause for self-pity.

It was about the same time that I said quite crossly to the Lord (yes, I was cross with him too), 'Just what is all this about dying to self?' It did not seem to be clearly set out in scripture—not the 'how' at any rate—and the current Christian clichés did not help me. Maybe God smiled and said, 'I'll show you', as indeed he did over the next few years. I was full of questions.

Must I really put my interests to death? Have I no rights? Must I abandon my career and my hobbies, blotting myself out for the sake of someone else? It sounds like some ghastly suicide, or like some chemical that leaches everything away, leaving only a flimsy shell. I don't want to destroy my personality. I don't want to be someone else's doormat.

Gradually I began to understand as practical experience and biblical insights complemented one another piecemeal. I began to see that God could ask us to serve because he himself is a serving God. The Father continually services the universe and keeps it going. The Spirit's chief function among mankind is enabling and serving. Jesus was, above all, the Servant, in all his dealings with the sick and needy, in all he taught, and most of all in his death. Moreover, his supreme servanthood was not the result of his being less than his Father, but a deliberate choice, knowing exactly who and what he was—one with God.

So if Jesus, who was one with the Creator of the universe, acted as a servant, then servanthood after his model is not a mark of inferiority but of loving obedience. Because he who is Lord of all was a willing servant, he may demand of us that we also should be willing servants.

SERVANTHOOD

[Jesus said to his disciples] 'Suppose one of you had a servant ploughing or looking after the sheep. Would he say to the servant when he comes in from the field, "Come along now and sit down to eat"? Would he not rather say, "Prepare my supper, get yourself ready and wait on me while I eat and drink; after that you may eat and drink"? Would he thank the servant because he did what he was told to do? So you also, when you have done everything you were told to do, should say, "We are unworthy servants; we have only done our duty."'

LUKE 17:7–10

Imagine the situation. A hired servant has worked hard all day in his master's fields and comes back tired and hungry in the evening. All he wants is a hot bath and a good supper. But his boss is also hungry. The boss doesn't go into the kitchen and prepare a meal for his weary labourer. Not at all. Seeing him come in, he says, 'I was wondering when you'd be back. Get yourself cleaned up, and hurry up with my supper.' Only after the boss has fed can the servant sit down for his meal.

How inconsiderate and unfair! Surely Jesus, as an exponent of social justice, must have commended strike action, or at least a complaint and a moan? But no. The boss, he says, will not even thank the servant, who was simply carrying out his duties. 'So you also, when you have done everything you were told to do, should say, "We are unworthy servants; we have only done our duty."'

For two or three years, some time before we moved in with her, Thursday was my day for visiting my mother. Leaving my own house in more or less disorder, I drove the three-quarter-hour journey to her house, and set about doing what was needed. At exactly five to one she would say, 'What about lunch?' because it had to be at exactly one o'clock. Did I say, 'I am an unworthy servant; I have only done what was my duty'? Far from it. My blood boiled. She was perfectly capable of getting lunch, putting the habitual bread and cheese on the table, but—'It's so nice to have a holiday from cooking.'

And I wasn't her servant, was I? I was her daughter, and surely that's different? Then I found some more uncomfortable verses. In Ephesians 5:21 I read, 'Submit to one another out of reverence for Christ.' Well, that could mean that my mother should also submit to me. Could I not expect some consideration? What about her changing some of her attitudes?

'You, my brothers, were called to be free,' I read in Paul's letter to the Galatians (5:13). 'But do not use your freedom to indulge the sinful nature; rather, serve one another in love.' And then it goes on to throw the burden on to me. It seems I may not demand obedience from others. My first responsibility is for me to be obedient. (Maybe this has something to do with removing the log out of my own eye before trying to tackle the speck in yours?) 'The entire law,' Paul continues, 'is summed up in a single command: "Love your neighbour as yourself." If you keep on biting and devouring one another, watch out or you will be destroyed by each other' (Galatians 5:14–15).

That 'bite and devour' rings a bell somewhere. 'You never do so-and-so,' one of us complains to another, or 'You always…'. It is seldom wholly true but it voices my frustration at the way things seem to be fixed. Do we lock each other into negative behaviour patterns by expecting them of one another? Did my tension, as I rushed round flinging lunch on the table and anticipating the 'When's lunch?', engender a similar tension in my mother, which in turn programmed her, reared to military punctuality for meals, into anxiety that lunch might be late or non-existent?

The situation was altogether too self-perpetuating and too full of tension to be right, but what was the way out? Again a Bible letter pointed the way. Peter writes in 1 Peter 5:5, 'You that are younger be subject to the elders. Clothe yourselves, all of you, with humility towards one another, for "God opposes the proud, but gives grace to the humble"' (RSV).

I take comfort from the 'clothing with humility'. If I were, by great effort of will, to negate my own self, to 'be unselfish', it would be a destructive thing and could lead to bitterness. But we are instructed to put on a humble garment, the garment that God himself wears. Letting go of my own selfish will so that he can clothe me in his way is constructive. Risky it may seem—after all, I know my way, and have learnt little as yet of his—but like all his paradoxes it promises to be creative.

Paul wrote a letter to Philemon about one of his slaves, Onesimus, who wanted to take the risk of going back to his former master. A big risk it was, too, for in the Roman Empire a master had the right of life and death over a slave.

We do not know how he became a slave, whether he was captured in war, sold by his family to meet debts, or even born into slavery. What we do know is that although his name means ‘Useful’, he was a pretty useless slave, and that he so much disliked being Philemon’s slave that he ran away. I guess that slavery was to him a cage in which he felt trapped. Resenting and resisting the cage, he had not the heart to work willingly within it.

But when he ran away, he met Paul, and through Paul he met Jesus. That changed things. Paul’s reluctance to let him go suggests that he had learnt to be useful, and although Paul asks Philemon to welcome him back not as a returned runaway slave but as a dear brother, the implication is that Onesimus now really will live up to his name.

It seems clear, too, that Onesimus wanted to go back to Philemon, even if in fear and trembling at what might await him. He wanted to go back to the situation that had formerly caged him. He could not know how Philemon would receive him, but he went willingly.

Caring for frail elderly parents can feel a bit like a cage. One is very tied. However good the support and help may be, the chief carer has a perpetual and repetitive responsibility. Even when you go out, it is all too easy to take the responsibility with you. One is, to a degree, trapped and caged.

But maybe if, like Onesimus, I go into that cage voluntarily, and willingly close the door behind me, I may find that it is no longer a cage, but home.

FALSE GUILT

On the third day, Joseph said to them, 'Do this and you will live, for I fear God: If you are honest men, let one of your brothers stay here in prison, while the rest of you go and take grain back for your starving households. But you must bring your youngest brother to me, so that your words may be verified and that you may not die.' This they proceeded to do. They said to one another, 'Surely we are being punished because of our brother. We saw how distressed he was when he pleaded with us for his life, but we would not listen; that's why this distress has come upon us.' Reuben replied, 'Didn't I tell you not to sin against the boy? But you wouldn't listen! Now we must give an accounting for his blood.' They did not realise that Joseph could understand them, since he was using an interpreter.

GENESIS 42:18–23

When famine swept the Middle East, Joseph's inspired forethought paid off, and from far and near people came to Egypt to buy the grain that he had caused to be stored from the good years. Among them came ten of his brothers, who bowed before him just as he had dreamed that they would. They had no idea that the man next in power to Pharaoh was their own brother. He led them a merry dance, accusing them of being spies, demanding that they bring Benjamin as proof of their honesty, and imprisoning them for three days.

Maybe it was because they were in Egypt that they connected their distress at the hands of this powerful man with their treatment of Joseph whom they had sold into Egypt. At all events their crime against him had evidently begun to weigh on their consciences.

Joseph piled on the guilt, because that guilt was real. They were being forced to admit their guilt and to take risks with their own lives by bringing Benjamin to Egypt—in the end it was a matter of do that or starve. Admitting their guilt, they were prepared to be punished for what they had done.

This is real guilt, the guilt from which Jesus died to save us. Real guilt is having done what should not have been done. It is having sinned. When an accused person is found guilty in a court of law, the court is saying, 'Yes, you did this wrong thing.' This is real guilt, for which Jesus has provided a way out, for 'there is now no condemnation for those who are in Christ Jesus' (Romans 8:1).

There is, however, false guilt. While it would be wrong to try to dodge responsibility for any real wrong that we have done, it is not right to take on a sense of guilt for any other reason.

False guilt can be built up by other people's expectations of us, whether actual or assumed. For me, I think it has come from my own expectations of myself. Once or twice my mother fell out of bed and I felt terribly guilty about the time she must have spent lying on the floor, accusing myself of neglecting safety precautions, of being an inefficient carer. It would have been better just to admit my mistakes and improve her security, not, as I did, to lash myself with guilt.

For a number of years we had hosted a house party for teenagers. It took place during the Easter holidays in a boarding school building about ten miles from my mother's home, and both my husband and I were very committed to it and blessed by it. The fact that we were now caring for my mother was not, we felt, a reason to give up doing it, but during the ten days of leaders' preparation and the house party itself, it needed our undivided attention.

God clearly answered our prayers when, for each of the last two Easters of my mother's life, a local nursing home was able to take her, due to an unexpected vacancy. God's answer—but I felt so guilty. The first year she was sharing a bedroom with others, which I assumed she would not like. My husband had to tell me to stop tearing myself apart about it and get on with what we had to do.

Some of the care was less than we would have liked. When we dropped in on our way to the house party to deliver something we had forgotten, young Saturday staff had allowed food to spill down her front and had not cleaned it up, and her blouse was untucked where her trousers were not comfortably pulled up. But when we went to take her home at the end of the week, we found her sitting in the day room holding hands with another resident, both of them beaming happily.

It is surely false guilt that leads one to say, 'I couldn't let you do that, I'd feel so guilty.' Does that guilty feeling come because I really do not need the offered help, or because I have a problem receiving help, or is it because there is a big 'You ought' in my life? I'm woefully good at accumulating things I ought to do, and I gathered a number of them while caring for my mother. Worthy enough activities in themselves, and needy enough people as they were intended to help, they were knotting me up. With nights broken by her needs, I was getting very tired and disheartened.

A dear friend alerted me to what was happening in a letter which I have kept for its wisdom and honesty. She wrote that I was allowing Satan (whose name means 'the Accuser') to make me submit to all sorts of pressures which he had labelled 'God's will for Alexine'. He was taking away my joy and freedom in Jesus by 'You ought'.

The situation was engendered by the kind of guilt that I don't think God wants us to carry. What may be a good thing to do in itself may not be appropriate at that particular time, or it may better be done by someone else. False guilt carries all sorts of burdens beyond what God intends. As my friend said, beware of 'a hardening of the oughteries'!

BLOOMING

This is the text of the letter that the prophet Jeremiah sent from Jerusalem to the surviving elders among the exiles and to the priests, the prophets and all the other people Nebuchadnezzar had carried into exile from Jerusalem to Babylon...

This is what the Lord Almighty, the God of Israel, says to all those I carried into exile from Jerusalem to Babylon: 'Build houses and settle down; plant gardens and eat what they produce. Marry and have sons and daughters; find wives for your sons and give your daughters in marriage, so that they too may have sons and daughters. Increase in number there; do not decrease. Also, seek the peace and prosperity of the city to which I have carried you into exile. Pray to the Lord for it, because if it prospers, you too will prosper.'

JEREMIAH 29:1, 4–7

Care can feel like an exile. Those first months of caring for my mother felt like that, and they felt entirely temporary. I did not belong, because I did not expect to stay. Either someone else would take over the care or my mother would die.

I was rebellious about the whole situation. Like the Hebrews in exile in Babylon, I resented what I was having to do, moaning to my husband in evening phone calls. If this was God's idea, I was not impressed. I was being obedient very unwillingly.

God has numerous ways of easing us into change or helping us towards altering our attitude. One way is to give us something to do. There was plenty to do in making my mother's house more workable and her more comfortable, once I started to look for it. We had disliked her house as a depressing museum, but now we began to 'seek its peace and prosperity'. I planted the garden and we ate the produce. We welcomed our sons' girlfriends and saw the elder one married. We became part of the church that my mother had long attended, and began to belong.

Another way that God affects our attitude is by a direct touch. A friend took me to a meeting about healing because she thought it would interest me, but God had intentions beyond my mere interest. The speaker encouraged us to expect God to heal, and when the talk was over, anyone who would like to be prayed for was invited to raise their hand.

I raised my hand because my shoulders were very stiff and sometimes painful. Two members of the team came to me and it was my shoulders that I asked them to pray about. One of them put his hand on my shoulder and he must have felt the tension, for he began to pray about anxiety. But then God took me by surprise—I began to get angry. In my mind's eye were the family portraits that dominated my mother's dining room, and I lashed out about these forebears, the ancestors, who I felt were hemming me in, keeping an eye on me, somehow an oppression of the past. A sense of family history is great, yet it all felt heavy on me. I suppose it could have been that having lost her nuclear family my mother had clung to them as all that she had left. I used to be embarrassed as she self-consciously explained them to visitors. Whatever the reasons, I got quite worked up about them.

As those two people, whom I had never met before, prayed for me, I felt as if a long, long root like a parsnip was being pulled out of me. The 'root of bitterness' referred to in Hebrews 12:15 suddenly had real meaning for me.

Being freed from it made a big difference, enabling me to deal more effectively with my own resentment when it arose, and in time I got quite fond of my ancestors and the obvious likenesses in different members of my family.

About that time, I read a book called *Bloom Where You're Planted*.[1] It said a lot to me. A seed blown by the wind or carried by a bird may land anywhere and, if it could think, it might well object to growing in that particular spot. The fireweed springing up on a derelict site could dislike its surroundings, yet once it blooms the dereliction is transformed into a haze of deep pink. The stonecrop, holding on to minimal soil between rocks, could wonder if the struggle was worth it, but once it blooms the rocks are spattered with brilliant little stars. However unpromising the situation, blooming is possible. I had been wasting so much energy wishing I was somewhere else, and rebellion is very tiring.

Long before Jeremiah and the exile in Babylon, Moses gave a wise instruction: 'You shall rejoice before the Lord your God in all that you undertake' (Deuteronomy 12:18, RSV). He added that we should serve God 'with joyfulness and gladness of heart, by reason of the abundance of all things' (Deuteronomy 28:47, RSV).

At first the rejoicing may be through gritted teeth, but joyfulness and gladness of heart are within our reach and our control, once we get the message.

OH GOD, WHY?

The righteous flourish like a palm tree,
and grow like a cedar in Lebanon.
They are planted in the house of the Lord,
they flourish in the courts of our God.
They still bring forth fruit in old age,
they are ever full of sap and green,
to show that the Lord is upright;
he is my rock, and there is no unrighteousness in him.

PSALM 92:12–15 (RSV)

This psalm takes me right back to the book of Job. If the righteous truly flourish like it says, why then are apparently good people suddenly consumed by painful cancer? Why do some dear old men and women limp into old age suffering all sorts of ills?

The debate is as fresh now as it was in the time of Job. On the one hand it is said that God is just and loving, and rewards those who do right. The evildoers will have their come-uppance eventually. Yet on the other hand the evildoers seem to flourish, and people like Job, whom God himself commended as being blameless and upright, a righteous man, go through really hard times. And who is righteous anyway?

At one time I had a prolonged struggle about what makes

a person righteous or 'justified', what commends them in God's eyes. My struggle partly related to Paul's own struggle expressed in his letter to the Romans, the struggle to discern the respective roles of faith and the law. But as much as anything the problem for me was the way that this epistle is sometimes interpreted. Despite the importance of God's laws, I had the impression that we were unable to keep them, that whatever we did we couldn't win. How could a just God be so unreasonable?

A.W. Tozer, in his refreshingly straightforward way, cleared the brambles for me. He pointed out that the weakness in us that causes us to disobey God is not an inherent inability but the weakness of our wills; not that we can't but that we won't.[2]

Way back in Deuteronomy 30:11 and 14, God said, 'For this commandment which I command you this day is not too hard for you, neither is it far off... But the word is very near you; it is in your mouth and in your heart, *so that you can do it*' (RSV, my italics). The trouble is that we don't, and although much of our life may be good, we have only to sin in one area for the whole to be contaminated. A clean white shirt can be sparkling clean, but mark it with the tiniest stain and it is no longer clean.

A number of just men walk through the Old Testament, people who were upright and godly, commended by God. Yet Paul says, 'None is righteous, no, not one' (Romans 3:10, RSV). Simply doing right does not earn us rightness with God. So what, I asked, made these Old Testament people righteous?

I searched through and found that all those people who were cited as being upright in the sight of God, from righteous Noah to Zechariah and Elizabeth, the parents of

John the Baptist, made the prescribed animal sacrifices. The sacrifices symbolised the death that they deserved, both as part of humankind and because of their individual sins, and which was being suffered on their behalf by the animal. Jesus was the ultimate, the final sacrifice for sin, and it is only as we enter into that sacrifice for ourselves that God clothes us with his righteousness.

The much-quoted half-verse from Isaiah 64:6—'all our righteous acts are like filthy rags'—comes in the context of a people busy with the externals but failing to relate to God. At the other end of the spectrum, the letter of James addresses those who so strongly emphasise faith that they ignore its practical outworking in good living. As always, it is a matter of balance, of keeping both sides in harmony.

John wrote, 'Dear children, do not let anyone lead you astray. He who does what is right is righteous' (1 John 3:7). Isaiah wrote, 'I delight greatly in the Lord; my soul rejoices in my God. For he has clothed me with garments of salvation and arrayed me in a robe of righteousness' (Isaiah 61:10). So the righteous are those who both act rightly and are clothed with God's rightness; who are planted in the house of the Lord and do the works that he has prepared for them to walk in.

And yet they suffer. They suffer partly because suffering is endemic to the fallenness of humankind. Jesus refuted the idea that misfortune and accidents necessarily result directly from the victim's wrongdoing, citing for instance the Galileans slaughtered by Pilate, and the 18 people killed when a tower fell on them (Luke 13:1–4). On the other hand, when misfortune and sin actually were connected, he linked them (for example, in Luke 5:17–26), and it is obvious to us that some misuse or abuse of our bodies leads to sickness.

Beyond a certain point, one has to stop saying, 'Why is this happening?' and consider 'How do I deal with it?'

'The righteous flourish... in the courts of our God... They still bear fruit in old age' (Psalm 92:12–14). In our garden we have a couple of very old, gnarled apple trees which still bear a crop of fruit. One reason for their productiveness is that over the years they have been regularly and sometimes drastically pruned. Useless or excess branches have been cut back, reducing their spread, letting in the light, enhancing productivity.

The fruit that God wants the righteous to bear is the fruit of the Spirit that Paul describes in Galatians 5:22–23. Among the qualities in that list is patience—a quality that is learnt through having to be patient. Then there is faithfulness, hanging on no matter what; and self-control, one of the hardest to learn, particularly in relation to other people.

The hard part is the pruning, which may come in many forms—the need to be patient, the hanging on, the temper-keeping, and not least in suffering and illness. God is the gardener and he allows the pruning so that even to the end of our lives, like my old apple trees, we may continue to bear his beautiful fruit.

FORGIVENESS

JOSEPH

[God] called down famine on the land and destroyed all their supplies of food; and he sent a man before them—Joseph, sold as a slave. They bruised his feet with shackles, his neck was put in irons, till what he foretold came to pass, till the word of the Lord proved him true. The king sent and released him, the ruler of the peoples set him free. He made him master of his household, ruler over all he possessed, to instruct his princes as he pleased and teach his elders wisdom.

PSALM 105:16–22

As Joseph plodded to Egypt with his Ishmaelite owners, his neck chafed by an iron collar and with fetters on his feet, he had reason enough for resentment and bitterness. His brothers had taken his beautiful coat, his father's special gift, the mark of his favour, and each cold night reminded him of its loss. He had been tired and hungry when he had eventually found where his brothers were pasturing the sheep, but they had thrown him into a pit as soon as he arrived, and then sat down to eat their lunch, as every pang of hunger now reminded him. He had heard their murderous designs; he had known powerlessness and fear. Then, though rescued from death, he had received the humiliating indignity of being sold—and, to make it worse, he was right.

He was right about his half-brothers' laziness on the job. His father had confidence in him. God had confidence in him, as those dreams demonstrated. He was the good one of the family, the blue-eyed boy, the specially favoured. Why should this happen to him? How unfair!

What turmoil there must have been in his thoughts! Demoted from favourite son to a slave up for sale, a nobody, he can hardly have seen this turn of events as for his benefit. How could he imagine that it was preparing a cocky teenager for future high destiny? He must have been tempted to sink down into rebellious apathy. But whatever his thoughts and struggles on the way, he had sorted out a good deal by the time he arrived in Egypt.

When he was sold to Potiphar, the Captain of the Guard, instead of sulking he set about doing as good a job as he could, and, having considerable ability, he was rewarded by becoming head steward of his master's household. He could also have become lover to his master's wife, had not God's law and God's will been central to his life. His refusal cost him his job, disgraced him and landed him in prison.

We cannot imagine the unpleasantness of an Egyptian prison. At least as a slave, even in irons, he had been moving about in the world, but here he was confined, shut away and at a gaoler's mercy. More testing, more lessons in obedience; more long, hard looks at self-righteousness; more training in servanthood; no doubt more crying to God, more learning to listen to him and to hear. As time went by, he again became the trusted servant, to whom the prison keeper committed the care of all the prisoners. He had hopes of release when a fellow prisoner, grateful for having a dream interpreted, was set free and reinstated, but the man forgot his promise for two whole years. No hint of bitterness is in the narrative, for by then it would seem that God had accomplished his purposes and Joseph had reached a point of humble acceptance of whatever circumstances God allowed.

All this time, twelve or thirteen years of training, Joseph had no contact with his family, and indeed did not see them for 18 years. How could he possibly be affecting their relationships one to another?

First and foremost, Joseph's 'death' and 'resurrection' and raising to glory foreshadow Jesus, through whom we can receive forgiveness and new relationships. Because Jesus left his heavenly 'family' and was willing to suffer for us and die for us, he can touch our lives and emotions at a deep level and literally resurrect them, bringing them into new life. What time alone can only blur, he can transform.

Mirroring this, if just one member of a family is living close to God, the whole family can be touched and transformed. One cannot but presume that Joseph prayed for his family and, as his own character was changed, prayed with decreasing self-interest and more and more for their own sake. Eighteen whole years—it makes my 'persistent prayer' efforts look pathetic. And as he prayed, he learned to forgive.

His dramatic rise to be controller of all the agricultural produce of Egypt gave him immense power, and when his brothers came to buy grain he could well have had his revenge. There are few more fascinating chapters than those relating his actions and emotions at that time, and certainly he tested his brothers to see to what extent they had changed, yet without any apparent animosity or desire for vengeance. At the moment when he finally revealed himself to them, he also spoke total forgiveness for them. (You can read the whole story in Genesis 42—45.)

FORGIVE ME

Then Peter came to Jesus and asked, 'Lord, how many times shall I forgive my brother when he sins against me? Up to seven times?' Jesus answered, 'I tell you, not seven times, but seventy-seven times.'

MATTHEW 18:21–22

'And when you stand praying, if you hold anything against anyone, forgive him, so that your Father in heaven may forgive you your sins.'

MARK 11:25

My mother understood about forgiveness. By her 27th birthday she had lost her entire immediate family. Her beloved father had died after five years of illness when she was in her teens. Both her brothers had met violent deaths, her half-brother shot while on a hunting expedition in India, her own brother murdered. Finally, medical negligence had contributed to her mother's death. She carried these sorrows through the next 30 years, until she received some teaching about forgiveness. Systematically, through Jesus, she forgave all the people who had caused those injuries in the past, releasing them from her own judgment to the judgment of God, refusing any more to hold their wrongs against them. And in forgiving, she entered into a new freedom and peace.

Not that she suddenly became perfect, and I was certainly not. There was a continued tension between us, and I was grateful that my husband's Army postings kept us living some distance apart. She was 80 when a local friend alerted us that she was becoming vague and neglecting herself and becoming too much for neighbourly helpers. In some trepidation I set out to spend a few weeks with her.

A train journey offers a good opportunity for prayer. As I travelled I asked the Lord about this problem and about our relationship. I was aware that I had often responded to hurt with aggression, and that I had not been an easy daughter to bring up. What he showed me now was that my mother and I were afraid of each other, afraid particularly of each other's sharp and critical tongues.

'Dear Father,' I prayed, 'thank you for showing me this. I am really sorry that I have sinned in this way. I've sinned against your law of love, and I've sinned against my mother. Please heal and take away this fear.' I knew that I could trust him to do this, perhaps instantly but more probably over time. His perfect love does indeed drive out fear, but it's clear in 1 John 4:18 that fear is also driven out by the growth of one's own love.

I could not just sit back and wait for God to do it; I had a part to play. It was important to act on what God had shown me and to do it promptly. Seeking my mother's forgiveness, being reconciled to her in this whole area of our relationship, was what I needed to do directly.

But what could I do? Her responses were slowing down and I was often unsure whether she took in much that was said to her. Discussing the issue was out of the question, yet it could not be ignored. I knew that somehow I must be obedient, and at once.

I took a taxi from the station and let myself into the house. My coat off, I went into the sitting room where she sat for so much of the day. I suppose it is pride that makes asking forgiveness so difficult, pride and fear of not being understood. Whatever the cause, I hesitated inside the door as she looked up without any particular greeting, yet I knew I could not delay. I went straight up to her chair, knelt beside her and asked her to forgive me for the rough way I had treated her over the years.

There was no visible response, yet I got up forgiven. Not only forgiven but I knew that the fear between us was gone. That was just the beginning for me.

PROS AND CONS

[King Solomon prayed] 'When [your people] sin against you—for there is no one who does not sin—and you become angry with them and give them over to the enemy, who takes them captive to his own land, far away or near; and if they have a change of heart in the land where they are held captive, and repent and plead with you in the land of their conquerors and say, "We have sinned, we have done wrong, we have acted wickedly"; and if they turn back to you with all their heart and soul... then hear their prayer... and forgive your people.'

1 KINGS 8:46–50 (ABRIDGED)

'Return, faithless Israel,' declares the Lord, 'I will frown on you no longer, for I am merciful,' declares the Lord, 'I will not be angry for ever. Only acknowledge your guilt.'

JEREMIAH 3:12–13

It has taken me a long time to accept that I am flawed. No, I didn't imagine that I had no faults. I recognised the faults and readily repented of them, but I was very distressed by their existence. Accepting myself as I am helps me to accept other people just as they are. It opens the way to real repentance, and to forgiving.

In neither case is this a matter of weighing up the pros

and cons and concentrating on the good points. Most of us have enough bad points to tip the balance, anyway! It is more about being prepared to admit that both the good side and the bad are me. Such an admission has become possible only as I have realised that I, the whole I, am acceptable to God through Jesus, that he takes me just as I am, and loves me just as I am, before he ever gets to work on any improvements. Since he accepts the (very) basic me, then so must I, and gradually I am learning to do so. Gradually the pride that hates admitting faults is dispelled by his unconditional love. Gradually the self-righteousness that makes it so hard to receive forgiveness is replaced by the knowledge that I am righteous only in Jesus, who loved me enough to die for me.

So it is with forgiving other people. Sometimes it seems as if one is faced not with forgiving any particular sin or fault or hurt, but with the baffling fact that they are who they are. Does it sound arrogant to say, 'I forgive you for being you'? Maybe it does, but that idea can contribute positively to learning to accept someone as he or she is, accepting the person, 'warts and all'.

I emphasise, 'the person'. I am not suggesting that we accept the sin that has been done either by myself or by another person. God does not do that. He challenges our honesty, challenges us to face up to wrong actions so that he may forgive and we may forgive one another.

Samuel Davies was a preacher in Virginia and North Carolina 300 years ago. He said:

You may be very sorry for your sin because it may fix a scandal on your character, because it may have injured your temporal estate, or because it may ruin you in the eternal world… and yet know nothing of true repentance. True repentance is a more kindly, generous thing; it proceeds from an affecting sense of the baseness and malignity of sin itself. True repentance is not focused on the sinner. It focuses, rather, on the fact that our holy, merciful and loving Father hates our sin and finds it repugnant.[3]

Throughout the Old Testament, God is saying that however far away we have gone from him, however rebellious we have been, we have only to turn wholeheartedly back to him and he will forgive us and take us into fellowship with himself.

In Isaiah 1:18 he says, 'Though your sins are like scarlet, they shall be as white as snow; though they are red as crimson, they shall be like wool.' Have you ever tried to get a bloodstain out of a garment? The longer it has been there, the more persistent it becomes. Even with biological washing powders it is very difficult to get out. It leaves a permanent stain. Yet God promises that forgiveness will make us like that marvellous whiteness of newly fallen snow, every blemish and dark part covered with shining white. His forgiveness is a complete wiping out of the record against us.

Some years after the forgiving that removed the fear between my mother and myself, my teenage daughter felt that there were other things in our relationship with my mother that needed clearing. It was after our family had moved in with her, and her senile dementia was more advanced than on the earlier occasion. Together my daughter and I knelt by her and asked her forgiveness. Again we knew the transforming power of being forgiven, both by her and by God.

NO EXCUSING

[Peter said to the crowd] 'The God of Abraham, Isaac and Jacob, the God of our fathers, has glorified his servant Jesus. You handed him over to be killed, and you disowned him before Pilate, though he had decided to let him go. You disowned the Holy and Righteous One and asked that a murderer be released to you. You killed the author of life, but God raised him from the dead. We are witnesses of this... Now, brothers, I know that you acted in ignorance, as did your leaders. But this is how God fulfilled what he had foretold through all the prophets, saying that his Christ would suffer. Repent, then, and turn to God, so that your sins may be wiped out, that times of refreshing may come from the Lord.'

ACTS 3:13–15, 17–19

If forgiving is not a matter of weighing up good and bad points and focusing on the good, then neither is it a matter of excusing. Never did God say to the Israelites, 'Oh well, I know you were living among all those pagans with their erotic worship. It was very hard for you, so I'll let you off.'

When Jesus, as he was being nailed to the cross, said, 'Father, forgive them for they do not know what they are doing', he was appealing not to extenuating circumstances but to the Father-heart of God. Those who crucified him did indeed not know that they were actually killing the Son of God. They acted in ignorance, but they still needed to seek forgiveness.

The enemy agent who murdered my mother's brother in 1918 was acting under orders in time of war, just as the Roman soldiers who crucified Jesus were acting under orders in an occupied country. In neither case does the excuse lessen the horror of the act.

That brother of my mother's, a brilliant inventor in his early 20s, had not long returned to England, glad to be back from the trenches in France. Always one to take part in amateur dramatics, he was dressing as a clown in preparation for an entertainment. Whoever it was who killed him came into his barrack room, silenced him with chloroform and then strangled him, a carefully planned, silent and macabre murder which the War Office at first hushed up. Local people gossiped that he had committed suicide, but then why was he buried with full military honours? Eventually friends of the family put pressure on the authorities to admit what had actually happened, and so quash the rumours that were exacerbating their hurt.

The hurt to those who loved him was devastating and deep. Excusing could not help them. What had been done was bad, very bad.

Whether or not the murderer himself ever sought God's forgiveness, my mother found that she had to reach the stage of no longer holding unforgiveness towards him in her heart. Whether or not a person who has injured us asks for forgiveness, whether or not they are known to have repented, we are not the judges. God is judge, and for our own health of both soul and body we are well advised to leave all judgment to him.

Omagh is a quiet town in Northern Ireland, lying between gentle green hills at the confluence of three rivers, a town where Catholics and Protestants lived alongside one another. This pleasant place became known worldwide on 15 August 1998. A community festival was in full swing when a car bomb consisting of as much as 300lb of home-made explosive blew up in the centre of the town.

Not content with the intended explosion, its perpetrators, a terrorist offshoot of the IRA, gave a warning to Ulster Television only 40 minutes before, saying that a bomb was close to the courthouse in Main Street. The police rapidly moved people away from the courthouse and down Market Street, where, as the terrorists knew, the car was parked which was due to blow up. By their apparent warning they had ensured that the maximum number of people was injured.

The bomb damage was totally indiscriminate. Twenty-eight people were killed, both Roman Catholic and Protestant, and eleven of those were under the age of 18, one a toddler killed with her mother and grandmother. Over 200 people were wounded, many of them critically. Among them was a young engaged couple just about to be married. Donna Marie was wheeling her niece in her pushchair when the bomb exploded. It killed the child and so badly injured Donna Marie that her father and brother walked past her hospital bed without recognising her—burns and shrapnel had injured two-thirds of her body. She was identified only by the engagement ring on her finger. Her fiancé Gary McGillion was also badly injured.

They spent 150 days undergoing plastic surgery, and for many months Donna Marie had to wear a metal and plastic head-frame to help the skin grafts heal that were reconstructing her face. Given only a 20 per cent chance of survival, she not only survived but got married to Gary within a year of the bombing. Though scarred, she was pictured in her wedding gown as radiant as if nothing had ever been amiss.

One clue to her recovery must surely be her attitude. She has been quoted as saying:

We said right from the start that we were not going to let the bombers turn us into bitter people. It would have been easy to feel sorry for ourselves and spend the rest of our lives full of anger and self-pity. I cannot change the past. All I can do is make the best of my future.

There were others too who lost loved ones and made headlines after that dreadful day because they spoke out forgiveness for the bombers.

Those terrorists, who called themselves the 'Real IRA', may never themselves arrive at a point of repentance. They may never enter into the freedom of God's forgiveness. That is their own choice. At least they are not held in bondage by bitterness in these people whom they injured, and who themselves have surely been blessed by their forgiving spirit.

HOW IT WAS FOR PETER

Then seizing [Jesus], they led him away and took him into the house of the high priest. Peter followed at a distance. But when they had kindled a fire in the middle of the courtyard and had sat down together, Peter sat down with them. A servant girl saw him seated there in the firelight. She looked closely at him and said, 'This man was with him.' But he denied it. 'Woman, I don't know him,' he said. A little later someone else saw him and said, 'You also are one of them.' 'Man, I am not!' Peter replied. About an hour later another asserted, 'Certainly this fellow was with him, for he is a Galilean.' Peter replied, 'Man, I don't know what you're talking about!' Just as he was speaking, the cock crowed. The Lord turned and looked straight at Peter. Then Peter remembered the word the Lord had spoken to him: 'Before the cock crows today, you will disown me three times.' And he went outside and wept bitterly.

LUKE 22:54–62

When Simon Peter denied Jesus, he was scared. He had already let Jesus down by falling asleep while he was agonising in prayer in the garden. Then, when the armed band came to arrest him, Peter had tried to defend him, but Jesus told him off for using the sword he had allowed him to bring. Stumbling after the soldiers' lanterns and torches, he had followed through the night as they jostled Jesus to the high priest's house. Only John was with him; all the others had run away. John, socially acceptable to the high priest's household, went right into the courtyard but Peter huddled outside the door. Then John nipped out and asked the doorkeeper to let him inside. But he didn't stay with Peter. He went indoors to hear what was going on.

Alone in the dark among total strangers, fearful of what would become of his beloved friend and Lord, forbidden to defend either himself or Jesus, terrified of being arrested as well, his one concern was to make himself inconspicuous. Yes, he was scared.

Jesus turned and looked at him with the love and sadness of his heavenly Father, and Peter wept. For the next three days he must have been utterly devastated, not only by Jesus' death but by his own failure and betrayal. And then Jesus appeared to him before appearing to any of the other apostles. He came to him privately on Easter Day (Luke 24:34).

We are not told what Jesus said to him, but from the way that forgiveness is depicted in the rest of scripture I would hazard a guess that he did not say, 'Well, Peter, at least you didn't run away like the others but followed me to the high priest's house (a good point), and I know how frightened you were (an excuse), so I'll forgive you.'

Nor did he say, 'That's all right, old man, it's nothing, forget it,' minimising what Peter had done.

No, I think he said something more like, 'Peter, you relied on your own boldness. You boasted and then you denied me three times. I saw your tears of repentance. I forgive you. Yes, you did this bad thing. Even if there is no excuse whatsoever, I will no longer hold it against you.'

The subject is closed, the sin wiped out. For the person doing the forgiving, this wiping out is an act of will. Jay Adams, an American who has written about counselling, wrote:

When you forgive someone, you are promising to do three things about his wrong doings. You promise:

(1) I shall not use them against you in the future;
(2) I shall not talk to others about them;
(3) I shall not dwell on them myself.

Just as the only way to begin to feel right toward another is to begin to do right toward him, so the only way to feel properly toward another, and ultimately even to forget those wrongs that he has done to you, is to keep the threefold promise that you make when you say 'I forgive you'.

You don't have to feel forgiving in order to grant forgiveness; you just have to forgive.

Jesus forgave Peter and wiped out the sin. Before long he offered him the opportunity to affirm his love and loyalty, asking him three times in different ways whether he loved him. Then, demonstrating that he no longer held Peter's sin against him, he gave him a personal commission. He gave him the responsible job of caring for all those for whom Jesus had cared and would care, and to truly become the rock on which the Church would be founded (John 21:15–19).

The simplicity of forgiveness almost offends us, that the simple act of asking to be forgiven, or of saying, 'I forgive you', can have such a real and deep effect. But that is the power of the word, the word spoken from the heart, and the power of God's promises.

RECEIVING FORGIVENESS

When Joseph's brothers saw that their father was dead, they said, 'What if Joseph holds a grudge against us and pays us back for all the wrongs we did to him?' So they sent word to Joseph, saying, 'Your father left these instructions before he died: "This is what you are to say to Joseph: I ask you to forgive your brothers the sins and the wrongs they committed in treating you so badly." Now please forgive the sins of the servants of the God of your father.' When their message came to him, Joseph wept. His brothers then came and threw themselves down before him. 'We are your slaves,' they said.

GENESIS 50:15–18

Quite as hard as forgiving can be receiving forgiveness, being really sure that we are forgiven. On the one hand we may be so ashamed of what we have done that we dare not believe it forgiven. On the other we could echo the child who said, 'But I'm nice!', an involuntary self-righteousness that cannot bear to admit the shadow side of our personality. Between these two lies a gamut of feelings and reactions, among them the fear that the forgiveness offered may not have been genuine, a fear that the forgiver is not trustworthy.

Panic on these lines seized Joseph's brothers when their father Jacob died. 'What we did to Joseph was so terrible, maybe he has been kind to us only for our father's sake.' So they fabricated a last paternal request, asking Joseph to forgive them because of Jacob and his God.

No wonder Joseph wept as they bowed down and offered themselves as his servants! A lesser man might have laughed, for here was the final fulfilment of the dreams that had so much angered them when he was a teenager. Here they were, bowing down before him like the sheaves of corn in one dream and the stars in the sky in the other. But Joseph's character was so in tune with God's that he wept.

Didn't they trust him? They had carried guilt concerning selling their brother for so many years before coming to Egypt, and now it all came up again. Despite the kindness and provision that Joseph had lavished on them, they were terrified that even now he would pay them back for what they had done to him so long ago. Yet there was no need for them to continue in this guilt. He points out that, however they may feel, God has turned the evil they intended to good, enabling many people to be kept alive through Joseph's economic management. God's overruling is part of sin's obliteration afforded by his forgiveness.

When my mother's life began to slow down in her late 70s, she would complain that she did nothing but read. Yet as time went by and her powers of communication gradually failed, reading remained a real occupation for her. Pages were sometimes torn, and her habit of folding paperbacks broke their spines.

One such volume was an early edition of the Good News version of the New Testament, which the bending treatment had reduced to three separate parts. From time to time she would spend a few days reading right through each part. We had no way of knowing how much her mind was comprehending until, in one of those periods, I learnt graphically that reading God's word still had power for her.

With two artificial hips and a very arthritic knee, she never knelt down, always in church receiving Communion standing at the altar rail. On this particular morning I went into the sitting room to find her kneeling at the sofa in the bay window. Her hands closed in prayer, she was saying, 'Forgive me, forgive me.'

I was somewhat nonplussed, not knowing what to do, so I just helped her up and settled her back on the sofa. But when I came back into the room a little later, she was again on her knees, again saying, 'Forgive me, forgive me.' Evidently this was important, and I would have to shed any embarrassment I might be feeling.

She knew that God forgives us when we repent and ask him to forgive, yet I could see that for some reason she now needed clear assurance that this was so. I did not at that critical moment sit down and work out the theology of the situation; the theology and practice were already clear in my mind.

Way back in my 20s, I had made a 'sacramental confession' in the presence of our church minister. On that occasion, not only was the voicing of the sin back through my life immensely important but so was the fact of priestly absolution. Over subsequent years, however, I learnt that the freedom and cleansing I had received in that instance were not just the result of structured confession in a church setting. The essential elements were real repentance and the declaration of forgiveness by a fellow believer who was listening to God.

In fellowship with other Christians who were learning to walk in the Spirit, I realised too the wonderful fact that Peter spells out in his first epistle, that we are 'a chosen people, a royal priesthood, a holy nation, a people belonging to God, that you may declare the praises of him who called you out of darkness into his wonderful light' (1 Peter 2:9).

A royal priesthood, able to intercede for one another. A royal priesthood, ready to confess our sins to one another. A royal priesthood who, like the disciples gathered together on the first Easter Day, have been breathed on by Jesus' Holy Spirit with the commission, 'If you forgive anyone his sins, they are forgiven' (John 20:23). As a member of the royal priesthood I was confident that I had the Father's authority to proclaim what has been done through Jesus, to declare that in him my mother's cry for forgiveness had been heard and answered.

So sitting beside her, I laid my hand on her shoulder and said, 'Darling, you are forgiven.' She relaxed and sat down again in peace. There was no confusion in her soul, and a vital transaction had been accomplished.

THE PERSON INSIDE

HOW SENILE IS SENILE?

Therefore lift your drooping hands and strengthen your weak knees, and make straight paths for your feet, so that what is lame may not be put out of joint but rather be healed. Strive for peace with all men, and for the holiness without which no one will see the Lord. See to it that no one fail to obtain the grace of God; that no 'root of bitterness' spring up and cause trouble, and by it the many become defiled [i.e. made dirty, polluted, corrupted].

HEBREWS 12:12–15 (RSV)

As old age diminishes the amount of 'doing' a person can engage in, the focus has to move to 'being'. Maybe that is an important function of growing old, to provide time to come to terms with the person inside, the person so many of us are at pains to conceal under what we think is a more acceptable exterior. For however much the 'outward man' decays, the permanent 'me' remains. Even if disease and changed body chemistry alter behaviour and slow down reactions, the essential heart or soul, the person inside, is still present and alive.

Old people often find a new freedom to say what is in their mind, which can reveal much if carers and family will only listen and discern. What is said may take the family by surprise. We didn't realise Dad had it in him to think that! Or, how shocking that Mum should react in this way!

All of a sudden, the parents we thought we knew are revealed in a new light, perhaps more human and flawed or more lovable than ever before, showing us new aspects of the person inside.

Out of the blue, Kate's mother said in an injured tone, 'When I came out of hospital, I had to make the tea.' Kate was flabbergasted. It was years and years ago that her mother had been in hospital, when she herself was still in her teens. Thinking about it, her first reaction was to justify herself. 'Dad and I were out at work. How could we make the tea?' Then she had to admit that perhaps they or the hospital could have made more considerate arrangements. Perhaps they could have laid a tray ready for her return. But all that time ago! To be brought up now!

Then her thoughts focused on her mother. What a burden of resentment she had carried all these years, which this memory was crystallising! Or had that incident said to her that she was not of any real significance? Either way, was there a clue here to her recurrent depression?

The Japanese author Yasushi Inoue has written a gentle book about the last years of his mother's life.[4] Her short-term memory kept fading, and he saw this as her gradually erasing from memory the latter years of her life. But to me his delicately told story suggests a different interpretation.

At one period she spoke constantly of two brilliant young brothers to whom she had probably been successively betrothed when she was still very young. Each had died at the age of 17. She spoke of them only to her grandchildren, who at the time were about that age themselves. Her deep love of the elder brother was clear to them all. Yet they were somehow shocked that she should talk so much of him and not of her late husband, a stern man with whom she had shared half a century. Eventually indeed she asked to be excused any further obligations to the memory of her husband, whom she felt she had already adequately served.

She must have been barely ten when her beloved died. Perhaps her parents, like many adults, discounted both the depth of her love for him and the strength of her grief. Perhaps neither emotion had ever been fully expressed. The husband eventually chosen for her was cool and even tyrannical. In her octogenarian widowhood she sought permission to cherish things as she longed for them to have been.

To have gone along with her could be thought of as encouraging fantasy, an unreal escape world. Or it could be that her speaking of her long-lost loves was an opening through which something good could have come.

An experienced carer once said, 'If an old person says to you "Oh, Mary...", don't say, "No, dear, I'm not Mary, I'm Doris." Just be Mary for a while, and allow the connection, the recollection, to surface. Go with it, and see what you can learn together.'

Old people are often not nearly as out of touch or confused as we think—as Joseph discovered with his father Jacob in Genesis 48. Jacob was terminally ill, already so weak that to sit up in bed was a big effort. His sight had almost gone with age. Only a few days before, he had made arrangements with Joseph for his burial, but now he seemed confused. Joseph was bringing his sons Manasseh and Ephraim to him for his blessing, for Jacob wanted these two grandsons to be on the same footing as his own twelve sons. Yet when they came in, was it confusion or near-blindness that made him say, 'Who are these?' Once he knew who they were, he hugged and kissed them, and then came the time for the blessing.

The custom was that the firstborn's blessing would be given under the right hand of the patriarch, the younger under the left hand, and Joseph placed his sons under the appropriate hands. His father, however, crossed his hands so that Ephraim, the younger grandson, was under his right hand to receive the firstborn's blessing.

Joseph was not pleased. 'He's past it,' he probably thought. 'He doesn't know what he's doing and anyway he can't see', and he took his father's hand to change it over, saying, 'Not so, my father, for this one is the firstborn, put your right hand upon his head.'

But Jacob knew exactly what he was doing. He was hearing what God had in store for these boys and their descendants. 'I know, my son, I know,' he said, and went on to explain. The family was fortunate that right up to the end of his life Jacob's mental faculties remained clear.

This special relationship that Jacob wanted for Rachel's grandsons whom she never knew, might this be a healing for the long-endured grief for her death? He links the two, saying, 'For when I came from Paddan, Rachel to my sorrow died in the land of Canaan on the way... and I buried her.' Maybe the expressing and the action were a major part of the putting right, the healing, that is needed as a person approaches the end of his life.

The casual observer sees only the outward decay of old age, but for the person inside that deteriorating body there can be development, growth and healing.

FACTS AND FEELINGS

The Spirit helps us in our weakness; for we do not know how to pray as we ought, but the Spirit himself intercedes for us with sighs too deep for words. And he who searches the hearts of men knows what is the mind of the Spirit, because the Spirit intercedes for the saints according to the will of God.

ROMANS 8:26–27 (RSV)

Discussing old photographs which jog memories is a popular and beneficial activity among the elderly. As more and more of their contemporaries die, there are ever fewer friends who share their history, who help them to know who they are in relation to people and surroundings.

Facts portrayed may bring back memories of feelings about the facts, and it is feelings that endure and shape a person, feelings about what happened. Sometimes an old person's remarks that seem confused or inconsequential may actually be like a door opening a crack to reveal emotions and feelings that need to be healed.

When Kate's mother complained about having had to make the tea, what she said was not essentially about the facts of her discharge from hospital. It was about how she felt about the facts as she perceived them, feelings that had been concealed for years.

Sometimes we deal with negative feelings by saying, 'I shouldn't feel like that', and we push them underground and try to produce in ourselves more acceptable feelings. The trouble with this is that a load of guilt comes with it. Guilt demands concealment, and things that are shut away tend to go bad. Somehow they need to be unearthed and healed.

Some carers have antennae sensitive to such interior needs. Others of us pick them up only as the Holy Spirit highlights a situation or a remark. In either case, turning the knowledge into prayer may be just what the old person was needing, prayer that does not necessarily have to be voiced to be heard and answered.

Every day for lunch an old lady had a banana, so they were a familiar sight. But one day she looked at the banana waiting on its plate and said, 'Horrible!' Her carer's knowledge of some of her marriage problems was focused by a nudge from the Holy Spirit. 'That banana to her at this moment is a penis.' And so the carer prayed healing for whatever memory and fear had been evoked in her soul.

When I first began looking after my mother, a struggle seemed to be going on in her face. She had always had a lovely smile but now, whenever she tried to smile, it was as if her face was being dragged down into a look of gloom. Her mouth was always pulled down at the corners, and her attempts to smile just produced an anguished look. I could have dismissed this as a result of one of her small strokes, but I sensed that there was more to it. Her misery in the lonely years since my father's death, not unmixed with self-pity, had become habitual, and we became aware of other factors as well.

Where to begin? We knew that prayer needs to be specific

and in accordance with God's will. So we asked the Holy Spirit to show us how to pray.

We sensed that her house was full of sorrow. It had been built in sorrow after deaths in World War I, and sorrow seemed to darken it still. Gradually we prayed through every room, and as we asked God to clear away the darkness and to fill each one with his presence, the atmosphere lifted.

From time to time we felt that God led us in praying for my mother herself. Often these prayers were about very little things. As she and I sat at meals alone together, she would make some odd remark and I would see quite clearly why, from the past, she was saying it, what it revealed. 'That,' I would sense the Holy Spirit was saying, 'is what I want to heal this time.' Silently I would say, 'Lord, please heal this,' and trusted that he did. It was a growth area for faith, as the evidence built up of her inner healing.

There was no need to agonise over the past, no amateur psychoanalysis, for the Holy Spirit touched each point with his unerring knowledge and, as he touched, it was healed.

One big problem was boredom. Naturally she who used to fill her days so full was often desperately bored. Yet there was more to it than just not being able to do very much, or lack of stimulus. In the years when I visited her weekly, I used to feel boredom descend on me like a pall. Living with her, it came every evening as we settled down after supper, a fear of boredom and then boredom itself.

The Holy Spirit impressed upon me that here was not just a need for finding things to do, humanly combating boredom. I felt that she was somehow oppressed in this part of her life by a spiritual power outside herself that needed to be defeated through Jesus' freely given life-blood. I think I was not even present with her when I prayed against a 'spirit of boredom'. There were, afterwards, times when my mother was bored. Who would not be bored when an immensely active life becomes constrained by physical limitations and reduced concentration? But the oppressive and irresistible sense of boredom was gone.

We saw God's victory when she began to smile.

THE LIVING SPIRIT

I cried to you for help, O Lord my God, and you healed me. You brought me back from the world of the dead. I was with those who go down to the depths below, but you restored my life... You have changed my sadness into a joyful dance; you have taken off my clothes of mourning, and given me clothes of joy.

PSALM 30:2–3, 11 (GNB)

In the person whose spirit has been kindled into life, that spirit can still respond when mental and physical faculties fail. Some people steeped in the Bible continue to be able to complete quotations when other conversation has entirely ceased—even, in one person I know of, in a terminal coma.

Mrs Outram was a fit 96-year-old whose short-term memory had gone as the brain cells operating it had died. When her relatives visited her, she did not know them but asked repeatedly for her own mother. Normal conversation just did not register.

But when her son said, 'It's Good Friday, when Jesus died on the cross,' tears came into her eyes and she said, 'Oh, he did, didn't he?'

'But then,' her son said, 'there was Easter Day...'

'And it was all right,' she smiled.

The real core of a person, where heart, mind, will and spirit operate, is not negated by failing powers. These are but the tools. Brain and body are the inner person's tools for the time on earth. When they wear out they are discarded but the real, inner me and my relationship with God remain.

That relationship will be unique for each person. My own family did not have a tradition of learning and quoting Bible verses or of talking much of spiritual truths, nor did we readily pray together. But wanting some fellowship for and with my mother in the last year of her life, I used to sing a hymn after I had settled her in bed. I was too caught up in the doing of it, feeling a little foolish at first, to know if it meant anything to her, and she herself did not speak at all by that time, but my daughter's observation was that Gran looked for it and appreciated it. Her inner being recognised and responded to what I sang.

It is by no means possible always to know what is happening. Only God sees what is going on in a person's heart, and our conjectures may be way off-beam. You don't have to be senile to find it impossibly difficult to express what you are feeling, the problems and hurts that cry out to be resolved.

For my friends Jack and Pam, nothing seemed to have been resolved when Jack's mother died—no reconciliation, no repentance, no forgiveness. Their relationship had always been bad. She would probably not have welcomed any daughter-in-law, for she looked on Jack as her own, and she thoroughly disliked the wife he chose. From the beginning she made life difficult for Pam and seemed bent on wrecking their marriage. Jack's defence was to keep away from her, so that her behaviour compounded the loss of her son. There had been no words of reconciliation when she died. Pam recalls how alarmed she had felt at simply buying her a new nightie when she was terminally ill in hospital, fearing how she would react to the one Pam had chosen.

Clearing up her papers after her death, Jack and Pam came upon a precious gift. It was poems and prayers that she had written. They expressed the sorrow and the desire for forgiveness and reconciliation that she had never been able to say directly to those two whom she had hurt. Finding them, Jack and Pam were allowed to know what had been in her heart in her later years, how much she regretted her actions and longed for redress, how much in fact she did love them.

Since her lifelong behaviour patterns had not altered, they had not guessed that there had been a change of heart. Of course they were sad that nothing had ever been said, that she had never brought herself to tell them what was going on. Together they could have had such rejoicing and reconciliation. But at least now their own forgiveness for her was released in them, and the relationship was in some measure healed, although she was no longer with them. Now they knew of her deep feelings and of the transforming that had been happening at the levels of permanent reality, in the person inside.

Some inner changes may come about through praying carers. In other instances they arrive through the internal struggles of old people themselves.

Patricia and Frank were not believers, but Patricia's mother Adeline was. Patricia had many problems to deal with following the stroke which left her mother lame and speechless. All she could say was 'Do, da, do, da.' She was angry and unhappy. Patricia found her very difficult, and Frank considered her and her needs an intrusion into his life with Patricia. But gradually things changed. Patricia writes:

My mother was much better. She no longer screamed and cried. She was alert and smiling. It seemed to me as though she had travelled through some tortuous hell and come out enriched with some knowledge unavailable to the rest of us. She radiated a kind of joy which was more than mere acceptance of her lot. I felt she had found something she had been searching for all her life and I knew too that having found it, she was prepared for death. She no longer feared it. Her radiance affected us all. Our whole house was filled with happiness and I marvelled daily at how this could have come about.[5]

IVY

Then he showed me Joshua the high priest standing before the angel of the Lord, and Satan standing at his right side to accuse him. The Lord said to Satan, 'The Lord rebuke you, Satan! The Lord, who has chosen Jerusalem, rebuke you! Is not this man a burning stick snatched from the fire?' Now Joshua was dressed in filthy clothes as he stood before the angel. The angel said to those who were standing before him, 'Take off his filthy clothes.' Then he said to Joshua, 'See, I have taken away your sin, and I will put rich garments on you.'

ZECHARIAH 3:1–4

Such sadness ran through Ivy's life that one might have expected her old age to be difficult. To escape the slavery of caring for four brothers and two sisters at home in Wales, she had trained as a nurse, later marrying an Irishman from a strict Brethren background. In the last year of the war, he was pushed into joining up, and was killed just before it ended.

Left with her young son Hugh, Ivy decided to bring him up alone, refusing any further help from their families. For the sake of having a home, she took residential jobs for which her nursing well qualified her, ending up in London as matron of a large home for old people.

It was while she was there that Hugh, now 29 years old,

married Chris. Ivy just could not cope with his belonging to someone else. She gave up her job and moved to Cardiff where she had a severe accident, falling from a first-floor balcony on to concrete and sustaining internal injuries. When she left hospital, Hugh and Chris, not yet married a year, looked after her for eight months before she moved into a nearby flat.

For 15 years she suffered from depression, missing the company, purpose and significance that working in institutions had given her. Then a severe stroke disabled her. Eating was the only thing she could do for herself, but she still had the power of speech. She used that to give vent to all her frustrations and anger. Discharged from hospital, she again moved in with Hugh and Chris and their two young children and a lodger.

Chris just could not like her as a person. She was such a difficult lady. On occasion she screamed, sometimes all day. After a while Chris began to suspect that some kind of tormenting spirit was afflicting her. She longed to be able to do something for her but she could see no way in. All she could do was pray, so she prayed, and prayed, on her own, for two-and-a-half years. Occasionally Ivy went to church with the family but her idea of God, from her strict Brethren upbringing, was one of judgment. She had no idea of his love and mercy.

One Sunday morning, someone came back after church who wanted to talk with Chris. No sooner were they settled down in the sitting room than in came the lodger saying, 'Grandma needs you.' It was the last thing Chris wanted. 'I've looked after her all week; I'm in the middle of a conversation. I've had enough.' But all the same she went.

Grandma, slumped in her chair as usual, said, 'I'm ready.'

'Ready? Ready for what?'

'Ready to repent. Isn't that what I have to do?'

Amazed, Chris led her in a prayer of repentance, and as she did so it was as if she saw the torment slide off her. Ivy changed dramatically, seemingly as relieved to be different as the family was to see the difference. But after only two days she was as bad as ever, tempting Chris to wonder if anything had really happened.

Then some days later Ivy was sitting in the kitchen. Suddenly she reached for a scrap of paper from the shopping-list pad and wrote on it, 'Satan, I don't belong to you now. Go away.' Evidently she needed to take hold of her new freedom for herself and actually to dismiss Satan from any part in her life.

From then on, she was free from the oppression. When Hugh suggested that perhaps the time had come for her to go into a nearby nursing home, Chris found herself strongly resisting the idea. A miracle had occurred in her relationship with Grandma and she really wanted to go on caring for this mother-in-law whom she now deeply loved. Reluctantly she agreed.

Six months later, Grandma died. Her funeral was a special occasion. Two people from the home who were present said, 'She was the most difficult person we have ever had, but we loved her.'

GOD AT WORK

Bless the Lord, O my soul; and all that is within me, bless his holy name! Bless the Lord, O my soul, and forget not all his benefits, who forgives all your iniquity, who heals all your diseases, who redeems your life from the Pit, who crowns you with steadfast love and mercy.

PSALM 103:1–4 (RSV)

Very rarely, an opportunity is given to glimpse how, when other powers are almost gone, the person inside is still relating to God. Such was given to John Sherrill as recounted in his book *Mother's Song*.[6]

Years before, his mother had made it plain that when the time came for her to die she wished to be allowed to die, with no 'heroic measures' taken to prolong her life. After she gave up her house, she had a room in a retirement home where she lived happily for a number of years. John was summoned there by the staff when, after some days of withdrawing from everyday life, she developed pneumonia. Although she was comatose and not expected to survive, they had attached her to an intravenous drip of glucose and antibiotics.

Remembering her 'living will' and the wishes she had repeatedly expressed, John immediately started to question in his mind this 'heroic measure'. Was this really what she would want? How did this situation differ from a previous bout of pneumonia when they had fought for her life? But it was her own actions that fully alerted him.

She had so belligerently resisted taking antibiotics orally and by injection that in order to keep the IV drip in her arms the nursing staff had tied her wrists to the bars of her cot. As she lay there, unconscious and mortally sick, she constantly tossed about, fighting to free her hands and sometimes moaning.

The conscious, reasoning, responsive part of her mind was inoperative and she did not react at all to her name being called, to clapped hands or to any other stimulus. But it seemed that her heart, her will, was intact, whatever was happening to her brain and body. A determined woman, she had long planned for a 'good dying', and her will fought against the denial of it, which medicine was forcing on her.

The Sherrill family, with understanding medical cooperation and after much agonising, decided that the IVs should be removed and all medication ceased. As soon as the needles were taken out and her hands released, Mrs Sherrill relaxed and was at peace. Her will could stop fighting and rest.

It was then that her soul, her inner awareness, was shown to be utterly alive. Her husband had been a minister, yet they had both always been reticent of talking about religious matters within the family, either in the way of discussing tenets of faith or of sharing spiritual experiences. John's father expected the Bible to speak for itself. His mother, observing how people who were vocal about their religious commitment often did not seem to match up to it in their daily lives, was wary of hypocrisy.

In his 30s the prospect of an early death from cancer had thrown John on to God, who, to his surprise, took him seriously, both healing the cancer and building up his new faith. He longed to share all this with his parents but his father died, and if he edged near the subject with his mother she steered the conversation away into safe, mundane topics.

They had had one illuminating encounter while she was still living in her own home. He was on a visit to her when early one morning she showed him her new verandah, which she called her 'thinking porch' and in which, she told him, she kept her Bible and private notebook. He hoped that at last she might be moving towards talking of spiritual things. He picked up her Bible and ventured a comment. Her response astonished him.

'People are always trying to manoeuvre me,' she said. As they stood facing each other in silence, John realised that she whom he had characterised as being a controlling person was herself terrified of being controlled.

They moved into the kitchen, John still holding her Bible. He put it on the counter and they had breakfast. Afterwards she fetched it and handed it to him, a gesture that was as near to an apology as she could bring herself. 'Read me a psalm, would you?' she said casually. 'It's my favourite book in the Bible. I'd like you to read for me.'

After her hands had been released and the IV needles removed, John sat beside her, chatting at first, but she was comatose with eyes fast shut. After a while he remembered that he had his travel Bible with him. Perhaps he should read to her from it, and yes! the Psalms would be right. He started to read Psalm 1: 'Blessed is the man who walks not in the counsel of the wicked.'

He glanced up at her occasionally, feeling somewhat awkward, and then to his astonishment he saw that her eyes were wide open—vivid blue eyes. She was listening, aware, with the intense alertness of a baby. 'You can't get in touch with a baby's mind,' John wrote, 'but you never doubt its awareness.' She made no response to any remark he himself made, but those eyes showed she was drinking in what he read in the book of Psalms.

Some passages were so apt that he could scarcely read them. 'The cords of death encompassed me... the snares of death confronted me. In my distress I called upon the Lord; to my God I cried for help. From his temple he heard my voice, and my cry to him reached his ears' (Psalm 18:4–6, RSV). The overall theme of those first few psalms seemed to be that of protection—protection not only for his mother but for him too.

The next day she was as unresponsive as ever to normal stimuli, but, as soon as John started to read, her blue eyes opened again. The theme that emerged was now one of repentance, and as he read Psalm 51 he looked up to see his mother's eyes filled with tears. 'Wash away all my iniquity and cleanse me from my sin. For I know my transgressions, and my sin is always before me' (Psalm 51:2–3). To his amazement, John was witnessing his mother doing business, a final cleansing, with her heavenly Father, the word of God dealing directly with her deep inner being, with the person inside.

He hardly dared to hope for this marvel of her alert, open eyes to continue the third day, but, as soon as he began reading, they were wide open. During that last afternoon he had with her, they did not stay open all the time but opened only at the psalms that spoke of praise and glory. Her hard business over, she was surely ready now for the glory to come. The final five psalms are a paean of praise and John could almost imagine that she was smiling.

A GOOD DYING

PREPARING TO DIE

Jacob lived seventeen years after his arrival [in Egypt], so he was 147 years old at the time of his death. As the time drew near for him to die, he called for his son Joseph and said to him, 'Swear to me most solemnly that you will honour this, my last request: do not bury me in Egypt. But when I am dead, take me out of Egypt and bury me beside my ancestors.' And Joseph promised. 'Swear that you will do it,' Jacob insisted. And Joseph did. Soon afterwards Jacob took to his bed.

GENESIS 47:28–31 (LB)

Then Israel said to Joseph, 'I am about to die, but God will be with you and will bring you again to Canaan, the land of your fathers.'

GENESIS 48:21 (LB)

When Jacob said to Joseph, 'I am about to die,' Joseph did not say, 'Oh no, Dad, I'm sure you've got lots more living to do.' He did not pretend that soon he would recover from his illness or that they could make plans for future days. He accepted that what Jacob said was true. He listened to what he had to say; he listened to his wishes. Then he followed his father's instructions to gather together all twelve brothers to hear his last words.

What an immense effort speaking those last words must have cost Jacob! He evidently chose to sit on the side of his bed (for Genesis 49:33 says that when he had finished he drew his feet up into the bed), perhaps in order to be able to put a hand on the head of each son. Maybe he had to be propped or held up.

Speaking partly from a lifetime's experience of his family, partly from what he had heard and was hearing from God, he spoke home truths over each of his sons in turn. He did not flinch from telling them things that must have been unpalatable, and some things that must have surprised them. The beloved child of his old age, Benjamin, got no special treatment but a short, telling word.

Having addressed all his sons, Jacob gave them exact instructions about his own burial. Then he drew up his feet into the bed, breathed his last (I wonder if this was the gasp as if for take-off that I witnessed in my mother?) and died.

It is surely easier to 'die well' if you know you are about to die. I suppose we all acknowledge in our heads that death is a future inescapable fact, although illogically I guess that we each have this odd feeling that it won't actually happen to us! Nevertheless, most of us do tackle it in the way of making wills and trying to sort our affairs and perhaps giving away belongings. But the final hours and days before death are quite another matter.

Tempted as relatives or carers to say nothing, we need to ask ourselves why we are keeping silent at this most important time. We claim that we do not want to upset the person who is dying, but may the more likely explanation be our own fear? We fear this final parting from someone we love, someone we have never before been without. We fear the process of dying, the reduction of every sign of living and the extraordinary cut-off point when that life is finally extinguished. And we fear death itself.

Although people are encouraged to witness the births of their children, few of us experience death at close hand. Loved ones are removed to hospital to be cared for by others, with anxious telephone contact in the hope of being present when death finally comes. Consequently, dying is no longer a natural part of living and has become a taboo subject. People are estranged from death and an awkward silence develops, often leaving a vacuum around the dying and bereaved.

Whatever may be our own fears and unanswered questions, the person moving towards imminent death has many yet more urgent. 'Why is this happening to me?' 'Why can't they make me better?' 'What sins did I commit to deserve this?' And when it is admitted that death is coming soon, what then?

A hospice nurse told me of a conversation she had with a retired farmer one morning while she was giving him his bath. He asked if everybody became as breathless and weak as he felt. When she had answered, he said, 'Never mind, you're going to make me better, aren't you?' She could not say 'Yes' because she knew it would not be true. What she said was, 'Well, we may not make you better but we certainly can make you feel better.' He was relieved to hear this answer because he knew she was giving him both honesty and hope.

Death is a completely alien experience, something that we have never done before, a place where we have never been before. And might there not even be a place? Might death mean a total snuffing out? But if there is a place, where will that place be? Will we lose our identity in some sort of spiritual merger? Will we return in another form? Is resurrection a reality and how can that be?

Many find great comfort in feeling that they will be meeting with loved ones who have already 'passed away'. But where have they passed away to? And will my credits be enough to cancel out my debits? Or can eternal life really be free?

If the gospel is true, if Jesus was indeed raised from the dead, if we have personal experience that he is alive and transformingly active today, then life after death, resurrection, is fact. As Paul wrote in 1 Corinthians 15:16–17, 'For if the dead are not raised, then Christ has not been raised either. And if Christ has not been raised, your faith is futile; you are still in your sins.'

How this certainty may be arrived at will be different for each person and reached by an individual route.

INTO THE LIGHT

But if it is preached that Christ has been raised from the dead, how can some of you say that there is no resurrection of the dead? If there is no resurrection of the dead, then not even Christ has been raised. And if Christ has not been raised, our preaching is useless and so is your faith... But someone may ask, 'How are the dead raised? With what kind of body will they come?' How foolish! What you sow does not come to life unless it dies... So will it be with the resurrection of the dead. The body that is sown is perishable, it is raised imperishable; it is sown in dishonour, it is raised in glory; it is sown in weakness, it is raised in power; it is sown a natural body, it is raised a spiritual body.

1 CORINTHIANS 15:12–14, 35–36, 42–44

I have witnessed few deaths but I have an unshakeable certainty that death is not the end. What Paul wrote is confirmed in so many ways. A few years ago I heard a BBC radio feature which brought together the 'near death' experiences of a number of people. The overriding common factor among them was awareness of great light, love and acceptance. And the light was often a person.

It was somebody (Kitto said), and I can remember rushing into his arms with tears streaming down my face, with a cry of joy in my heart, a sort of instant recognition. It was like running into the arms of a beloved father, and it was the sort of way that a father would embrace a child. And I remember a wonderful feeling of coming home. I didn't recognise him as such, and yet he was tremendously familiar. He related to me as just total love, total understanding, total acceptance.[7]

My father died aged 91 when we were in Germany. It was Whitsun and we were camping miles away from anything English. After we had settled the children in the tent, my husband and I switched on the car radio for the news, which came courtesy of the British Forces radio network. In a newsflash before the bulletin, we heard an SOS—for me! We dashed to the campsite warden's house and in our halting German asked if we might phone the number given. It took an age to get through. When at last we reached the duty officer, he told us that my mother had been frantically trying to contact me, for my father had pneumonia and was expected to die.

The Army was amazing and within 24 hours I was beside his bed in the hospital near my parents' home. He was no longer conscious and I was saddened by the array of tubes attached to him. My brother joined me and we prayed, thanking God for all that our beloved father had meant to us both. The next morning the hospital phoned to say he had 'passed on', which seemed, for once, an appropriate phrase—he had simply slipped from unconsciousness into the next life.

Most precious was what my brother told me. He had been at the house when my father was already ill but not yet in hospital. The minister brought Communion, which the four of them shared, and my father said with some glee, 'I'll be there before the lot of you!'

My mother had been distressed that once he was in hospital he did not seem to know her. He called out 'Ernest!' and an employee called Ernest assumed that this referred to himself and paid a fruitless visit. In fact my father had had a close and almost telepathic relationship with another Ernest, his own brother. He had died some years before, and my own feeling is that our loving heavenly Father had sent that Ernest along to welcome and encourage his brother into his new sphere of living.

For I am certain that we shall remain recognisably ourselves. Paul wrote to the Corinthians about the new bodies we shall be given, and I quote again from the BBC feature:

I found myself out of my body, floating up against the ceiling in a corner of the room, looking down on myself. What I was looking at down there was rather like a sort of nice old coat that I'd had for a very long time, which had given me years of good service, which was now very old and worn out, and was time to be discarded, and I needed to move on and find a new coat. And I felt totally peaceful and totally happy. I don't remember thinking, 'Oh gosh, I've got a body', and yet at the same time I was aware that I had a kind of form, and I had a shape which was me. I knew I was more intact, more whole, more myself, than I'd ever been before.[8]

My mother's going reinforced this for me. During the last week of her life I should have been leading a camp for disabled girls, but I was smitten by a virus which kept me in bed for several days and left me very weak. The first afternoon that I was up again I spent in the sitting room with her, she lying on the sofa. Looking across at her, I felt a great love for her, a deep love resulting from the four years we had had together, so much so that I had to go across and put my arms around her and tell her how dearly I loved her.

That evening we put her to bed and my husband left me to tidy up. All at once she half sat up with two big gasps—as if, I felt, for take-off—and then lay back. Only minutes later, as we looked at her together, we knew that she was gone, and that what we were seeing was an empty shell. The person had, in the old parlance, departed, no longer having need of this worn-out body. She was gathered to the people she had so sadly lost over the years, and to her Lord, and like the Old Testament patriarchs, we laid the shell to rest.

A TIME TO DIE

There is a time for everything, and a season for every activity under heaven:

a time to be born and a time to die,
a time to plant and a time to uproot,
a time to kill and a time to heal,
a time to tear down and a time to build,
a time to weep and a time to laugh,
a time to mourn and a time to dance.

ECCLESIASTES 3:1–4

But I trust in you, O Lord; I say, 'You are my God.' My times are in your hands; deliver me from my enemies.

PSALM 31:14–15

You do not have to hate someone to wish for them to die. Watching them day by day, you may feel that their life is a pointless burden and it would be better if, like a dog, they were 'put out of their misery'. Indeed some who are terminally ill may long for euthanasia.

On the other hand, medical interventions can impose difficult choices, for bodies can be kept alive unnaturally long. Wretched at the prospect of parting with someone we love, the human reaction can easily be, 'Do whatever you can.' Sensitive antennae are needed to get it right.

As her life ebbed away, my own mother ate less and less, and then she seemed to be unable to drink. Seeing her dry mouth, I tried to give her a few drops of water but it just dribbled out again. In a similar situation the parent of a friend of mine was put on a saline drip in hospital and kept alive for another month. Thinking of how, in the normal way, thirst really drives us to seek something to drink, I asked a doctor about this. His reply was that without liquid intake, urea builds up in the person's body and acts as an anaesthetic so that they are not in fact suffering. Ceasing to eat and drink is just the natural 'shut-down' process before the final end.

Sensitivity is certainly needed. Someone I know had been visiting a friend who was terminally, painfully ill. Driving home, she cried out to God in her distress, 'Lord, heal her or take her!' The reply came almost audibly: 'Don't ever ask that again. You do not have any idea what I am doing in that life at this time.'

We do not know all that is happening. We cannot play God. Yet at the same time he may indicate that positive rescue action is required. What appears to be impending death may not be his timing.

My friend Angela was a doctor, unable to practise because of caring for her ex-missionary mother, who was senile and incontinent. Incontinence can be the last straw for the carer. It was the middle of the night and yet another soaking wet bed had to be changed. Miserable, lonely, ashamed, with her mother waiting in a chair beside the bed, Angela vented her fury on the sheets and blankets.

Suddenly something made her look at her mother. She was blue in the face and gasping for breath as if she had pneumonia. Had the cold of the wet bed affected her that badly? What on earth was going on? Angela racked her brains for some medical explanation and, as she cast desperately around in her mind, it occurred to her that the problem might not be medical at all but spiritual.

Unlikely as it seemed, she had the feeling that the enemy of souls was trying for some reason to engineer her mother's death before the time was ripe, before God's time. It was as if a spiritual battle was going on around her.

Somehow they needed to be out of the room with the wet bed and all the angry feelings. As quickly as she could, she led her mother into another bedroom and sat her down. She laid her hands on her mother's head, all her fury now turned against the enemy. 'You're not going to take her in this way!' she cried.

Almost against her will she started to pray in tongues. At last her mother, still blue, gave a great sigh and said, 'Oh, that's better, thank you so much.' Gradually her colour returned to normal and she went quietly to bed. She lived for another two years and died in peace.

LISA

[Jesus said] 'I am the good shepherd. The good shepherd lays down his life for the sheep. The hired hand is not the shepherd who owns the sheep. So when he sees the wolf coming, he abandons the sheep and runs away. Then the wolf attacks the flock and scatters it. The man runs away because he is a hired hand and cares nothing for the sheep. I am the good shepherd; I know my sheep and my sheep know me–just as the Father knows me and I know the Father—and I lay down my life for the sheep. I have other sheep that are not of this sheep pen. I must bring them also. They too will listen to my voice, and there shall be one flock and one shepherd.'

JOHN 10:11–16

Lisa's parents were German Jews. Her grandmother had been killed in the gas chambers at Auschwitz and her father had been in Buchenwald concentration camp. Her mother managed to leave Germany and eventually, by a series of miraculous events, the two were united in England. They married, had three children and made a life for themselves, a hard life made worse by unhealed emotional wounds from Nazi Germany. Germany and religion were taboo subjects.

When Lisa found what she had long searched for—the

belief that God existed and that Jesus had died for her sins—her parents were tolerant and even happy for her but did not recognise her findings as something that they wanted or needed. She talked to each of them on various occasions (their marriage was not happy and they had separated) but eventually she had to leave it to God to water the seeds she had sown.

Six years later she had a serious argument with her mother, and had not seen her for some months when her mother was suddenly taken seriously ill. Lisa rushed to the hospital to be there as she came out of the operating theatre. They quickly resolved their difference and her mother said she had felt a kindly 'presence' while still conscious in the theatre.

As she got stronger, however, she pushed away that experience. Lisa had a family holiday already arranged and had to leave. In parting she gave her mother a card of the 'Footprints' poem, which tells of a dream of walking along the beach with God. As they walk through the scenes of the poet's life, so two sets of footprints are left behind in the sand. But then the poet notices that at times, when life got really tough, there was inexplicably only one set of prints. She asks God why he apparently deserted her when she most needed him. He replies, 'My precious, precious child, I love you and I would never, never leave you during your times of trials and suffering. When you see only one set of footprints, it was then that I carried you.'[9]

On holiday Lisa prayed for her mother a lot of the time. Praying, she seemed to be given a choice as to how to pray. She could pray for healing and a longer life for her mother, with the risk that she would again reject God, or she could pray that the Lord would meet her in her illness and she would know salvation. Lisa realised that she might have to sacrifice having her living longer in order to be together in eternity.

She chose to pray that God would meet her even if that meant her death. By the end of the week, news came that she had died.

When Lisa returned from holiday for the funeral, her sister thrust an exercise book into her hands: 'Here, this would interest you.' It was a diary her mother had kept of the last three weeks of her life. Intensely excited, Lisa read it into the small hours of the morning. She read that in her great pain and suffering her mother had indeed experienced God's love. 'Footprints' had impacted her life, and the care of the hospital staff showed her a love beyond the natural. She had shed bitterness and forgiven the lady with whom her husband had lived for many years after their unhappy marriage came to an end. She had found what she had longed for.

The funeral somehow confirmed that all was well. Because of the partly Jewish nature of the family and their rejection of all religion, Lisa's sister had given clear instructions to the funeral directors that this was to be a completely non-religious affair. However, something mysteriously 'went wrong' and Lisa and her husband quickly realised that they were attending an outright Christian service, the funeral of a 'child of God'. Aunts were furious, only mollified by the funeral director's reassurances of a mistake. But to Lisa and her husband it was a joyful confirmation of her mother's salvation and God's overruling.

Meanwhile Lisa continued to pray for her father, a hurt, volatile, ambitious workaholic. Having retired from business at 77, he mellowed as he adjusted to uncongenial leisure. But only two years later he had a stroke which robbed him of speech, a devastating blow. He hated having to allow people to see him helpless and degraded, to allow them to care for his most intimate needs. No spiritual change was evident in his life.

Only two months before the stroke, Lisa had found her prayer changing. She felt that God was telling her to stop praying 'asking' prayers for her father, and to start thanking God for him. Some time later, for some reason, she began asking again and felt all wrong inside until she remembered that she had been told just to give thanks for him, and once more stopped her petitions.

He did not have long to live. With two other people, Lisa asked God to confirm that her father now belonged to him by taking him on her birthday, 26 May. She waited, her faith stretched to the limit. Around 7.30 a.m. on 26 May she received news that he had died that morning.

MAUREEN

Dear friends, let us love one another, for love comes from God. Everyone who loves has been born of God and knows God. Whoever does not love does not know God, because God is love. This is how God showed his love among us: he sent his one and only Son into the world that we might live through him. This is love: not that we loved God but that he loved us and sent his Son as the one who would turn aside his wrath, taking away our sins. Dear friends, since God so loved us, we also ought to love one another. No one has ever seen God; but if we love each other, God lives in us and his love is made complete in us... There is no fear in love. But perfect love drives out fear, because fear has to do with punishment. The one who fears is not made perfect in love. We love because he first loved us.

1 JOHN 4:7–12, 18–19

Jesus [said], 'I tell you the truth, everyone who sins is a slave to sin. Now a slave has no permanent place in the family, but a son belongs to it for ever. So if the Son sets you free, you will be free indeed.'

JOHN 8:34–36

My friend Maureen told me how God's love for her had enabled her father to enter into that love.

Her father abused her as a child and young adult, besides giving her mother a hard time. Over the years Maureen had received much healing from God, but, because a physical condition, which she thought had been healed, had recurred, she went to a healing service. There she felt God say, 'You have been healed of that; just receive my healing.' She responded as best she could and so she was surprised when she felt that God was telling her to go forward for prayer. 'But why?' she said. 'I receive your healing.' However, she obeyed, and she and the person praying for her waited to see what God would bring to mind. What he brought was bitterness—bitterness towards her father.

That was Sunday. Through the following week, Maureen felt bathed in God's love, wave upon wave of it. At her Bible study group on the Thursday, she told the others how God had been talking to her about forgiveness. When she arrived home she prayed, and once more God bathed her in his love, but this time there was a definite command: 'Go and phone your father and tell him you love him.'

It was God's timing, for her father was intending to phone her himself to arrange for her to take him to a hospital appointment the following Monday. They made the arrangements and then with a great effort Maureen said, 'I want you to know that I love you' and put the phone down.

On the Monday, as she was driving him to the hospital, she told him how she had been wrestling with forgiving someone—she did not say whom. At this her father broke down in tears. He said that over the weekend God had spoken to him for the first time in his life, asking him to go to his wife (Maureen's mother) and ask her forgiveness.

He had gone to her bedside, knelt down and woken her and asked her to forgive him for all the wrong he had done her. He had always said that although he acknowledged God's forgiveness he could not forgive himself. But now he knew that he was forgiven.

In the car as he wept, Maureen reached over and touched him, an unfamiliar gesture. Doing so, she felt God's forgiveness flowing through to him.

Later that week, her brother saw him and said he was a different man, free and at peace and ready to die. He died at the end of the week.

MRS WILKINS

[Jesus told a story to illustrate God's generous grace.] 'The kingdom of heaven is like a landowner who went out early in the morning to hire men to work in his vineyard. He agreed to pay them a denarius for the day and sent them into his vineyard. About the third hour he went out and saw others standing in the market-place doing nothing. He told them, "You also go and work in my vineyard, and I will pay you whatever is right." So they went. He went out again about the sixth hour and the ninth hour and did the same thing. About the eleventh hour he went out and found still others standing around. He asked them, "Why have you been standing here all day long doing nothing?" "Because no one has hired us," they answered. He said to them, "You also go and work in my vineyard."

'When evening came, the owner of the vineyard said to his foreman, "Call the workers and pay them their wages, beginning with the last ones hired and going on to the first." The workers who were hired about the eleventh hour came and each received a denarius. So when those came who were hired first, they expected to receive more. But each one of them also received a denarius. When they received it, they began to grumble against the landowner. "These men who were hired last worked only one hour," they said, "and you have made them equal to us who have borne the burden of the work and the heat of the day." But he answered one of them, "Friend, I am not being unfair to you. Didn't you agree to work for a denarius? Take your pay and go. I want to give the man who was hired last the same as I gave you. Don't I have the right to do what I want with my own money? Or are you envious because I am generous?" So the last will be first, and the first will be last.'

MATTHEW 20:1–16

My friend Sue told me of a very special experience with one of her patients.

As a Marie Curie nurse, Sue was one of a rota of nurses caring for cancer patients in their own homes. She would arrive at ten o'clock in the evening and stay through the night, enabling the spouse or regular carer to have an uninterrupted night's sleep.

Mrs Wilkins was unconscious. Sue knew nothing about her except what was written in the nursing notes—that day after day she had been unsettled and restless. Mr Wilkins went to bed and silence enveloped the house, only disturbed by Mrs Wilkins' restless tossing.

Sue sat beside her bed, holding her hand, on her own in the silence. Gradually she became aware that Mrs Wilkins was struggling with fear. She sensed the pain in her of things not being resolved, of not knowing how to die. She sensed that this lady was afraid to cross the threshold between life and death.

As a nurse she was not supposed to talk about religion, nor did she want to take any advantage of her patient's vulnerability. She had to be careful. So she sat beside the bed, holding Mrs Wilkins' hand, praying silently and asking God what she could do to help her in her fear. She was perplexed because her patient could not respond or communicate what was going on in her heart and mind.

Eventually Sue spoke quietly to her. 'I don't know what you think about Jesus in any way. Maybe you haven't thought about this before. But one thing you can know about Jesus is that he has been through what you are going through. And if you want to, you can put your hand in his hand just like you've got your hand in mine, and he will be able to take you through anything.'

'I was giving her a choice,' Sue says, 'that she didn't know she had.' Mrs Wilkins kept hold of Sue's hand and after a while she relaxed and allowed Sue to straighten the bedclothes and pillows to make her comfortable. Sue went out of the room to let her sleep. When, after a little while, she went back to her, she had died.

She had been given a simple way to make her peace with God.

JEREMY

For you, O Lord, have delivered my soul from death, my eyes from tears, my feet from stumbling, that I may walk before the Lord in the land of the living. I believed even when I said, 'I am greatly afflicted.' And in my dismay I said, 'All men are liars.' How can I repay the Lord for all his goodness to me? I will lift up the cup of salvation and call on the name of the Lord. I will fulfil my vows to the Lord in the presence of all his people. Precious in the sight of the Lord is the death of his saints. O Lord, truly I am your servant; I am your servant, the son of your maidservant; you have freed me from my chains.

PSALM 116:8–16

I first met Jeremy and Fiona when I was in my 20s and living with my parents. They were to me the kind of friends that are tremendously valuable to a young person, a couple who were younger than my parents and older than myself. With one or two others we met weekly to read and discuss the Bible, growing in our understanding, and indeed our growth continued in parallel after I married and moved away. Once, when I was over from Germany, I visited Fiona and we were thrilled to learn that we had each experienced baptism (or 'inundation') in the Holy Spirit. What had begun as a social visit concluded with prayer, which, through Fiona's discernment, was one of the milestones in my own growth.

Knowing their love for the Lord and their constant walking in his ways, it was a wonderful blessing to hear of the manner of Jeremy's death.

At 76, he had recently celebrated his golden wedding. He and Fiona had married young, so they weren't your classic golden wedding couple—they were full of vigour as they planned the party. He chuckled as he told me that when they were discussing the plans with the caterers and asked them if they could manage tea as well as lunch and a drinks party and supper, the caterers said, 'It's not us we're worried about, but can you manage it?'

All was well, a lovely happy day, after which they went for a two-week holiday. While they were away, Jeremy began to feel unwell, though there was no obvious reason. He got no better once they were home. All too soon he was diagnosed as having cancer of the liver.

A nurse at the hospital told Fiona it was inoperable and she promptly said there should be no more tests, for they caused him much distress. Feeling that the doctor would be the best person to put Jeremy in the picture, she asked her to tell him, but either she did not do the telling very well or Jeremy simply hadn't taken it in, so it was Fiona who in the end had to make it clear.

Clear as it was, he could not at first accept the news. The hospital was suggesting hospice care. 'But,' he protested, 'no one ever comes out of the hospice alive!'

Have you ever been made redundant? Have you ever been evicted from your house? Has a relationship ever suddenly broken down? Whatever the cataclysm, we need time to get over the initial shock before we can begin to believe that the drastic change is true. And the most final cataclysm is impending death.

So Jeremy needed time to face up to the fact that he was going to die. In God's timing the hospice committee met the very evening that the diagnosis was confirmed, and he was able to move in there the next day. Fiona could not physically have looked after him at home—he was a big man, 6ft 4ins tall. In retrospect she valued having professionals in charge, and that not being constantly called upon she was able to remain fresh and untired.

The doctors were amazed that he died within three days. First of all, his children and grandchildren visited him. He asked Fiona to get him a wad of £10 notes, which he hid under his pillow. Then, as each of his grandchildren came to say goodbye, he gave them one apiece as a parting present.

After that, close friends, people who had been members of their couples' group and prayer groups, were invited to come in for a short time. Each kissed him and said some quiet word very briefly. Traditionally such a time has been thought of as a chance to make your peace, but Jeremy had kept short accounts and really there was no peace to be made—it was there already.

'I've said all the goodbyes,' he said then. 'I'm ready. Why am I still alive?'

He did not have long to wait. Calmed by sensitively gauged medication, he passed the evening with his wife, daughters and one of his sons-in-law sitting beside him, talking, reminiscing, even laughing at times. One daughter was reading a psalm about walking with God and trusting him, just as he gave three big sighs and died. Fiona committed him into the hands of the Lord, sending him on his way with her hand on his head. That is the kind of way that I would like to go.

MOURNING

When Jacob had finished giving instructions to his sons, he drew up his feet into the bed, breathed his last and was gathered to his people. Joseph threw himself upon his father and wept over him and kissed him. Then Joseph directed the physicians in his service to embalm his father Israel. So the physicians embalmed him, taking a full forty days, for that was the time required for embalming. And the Egyptians mourned for him seventy days.

When the days of mourning had passed, Joseph said to Pharaoh's court, 'If I have found favour in your eyes, speak to Pharaoh for me. Tell him, "My father made me swear an oath and said, 'I am about to die; bury me in the tomb I dug for myself in the land of Canaan.' Now let me go up and bury my father; then I will return."' Pharaoh said, 'Go up and bury your father, as he made you swear to do.' So Joseph went up to bury his father... When they reached the threshing-floor of Atad, near the Jordan, they lamented loudly and bitterly; and there Joseph observed a seven-day period of mourning for his father.

GENESIS 49:33–50:7, 10

We had a long preparation time for my mother's death, and, as a good friend pointed out to me, I had done most of my mourning before it occurred. Unlike a sudden death, which catapults us straight from having a whole, living, functioning person to nothing, I had seen her gradual deterioration over time. I had watched the reduction of her powers and her abilities, her means of expression, until only the essential being, like a fragile moth just waiting to flutter away, was left.

We had mourned the loss of her quick concerns, her eagerness for action to remedy wrongs, her wide enthusiastic interests. We had mourned the passing of her ability to paint, both her manual dexterity and her creative eye. We had said goodbye to the characteristics that we disliked, and had learnt to forgive.

Nevertheless, mourning cannot be skipped. However collected one may remain through all the business following a death, even through the funeral itself, weeping is necessary. In particular, I remember sitting talking with my brother some weeks afterwards and for the first time really weeping, not for any reason that I could acknowledge in my head but realising that I had not released the tears before and that they needed to come. Our shared history, my brother's and mine, and all that we had shared during our mother's care, made that release possible and appropriate.

When my father died and I was signally failing, indeed not even trying, to help my mother to mourn, an older friend called. I was alone and all I remember her saying as she offered her sympathy was, 'I know it all.' Inexplicably, this breached the dam of all my efficient coping and the tears flowed. There were other occasions later when I cried, but that was the first and necessary release.

Mourning is much more complex and difficult when a relationship has been bad, without the blessings of forgiveness. Sally told me how she and her sister had cared for their mother in turn. Their mother spent all Sally's turn moaning at her, and then, when it was her sister's turn, complained about Sally. Although she had inklings of the reasons behind this, Sally was constantly hurt. She was relieved when her mother died—and then she felt guilty that she should be relieved.

There will always be regrets, sometimes small but needle-like in their power. I have only to put the cover on a certain duvet to regret that I ranked the preservation of the bedlinen above my mother's comfort. A friend had given me for her this warm, light, goosedown duvet together with a good-quality cover. My mother had already torn several sheets by sucking or biting them with her sharp, pointed teeth. Unsure whether the duvet was a gift or a loan, and afraid that the cover would suffer the same fate, I did not use it for her. My mother would have been very much cosier and more comfortable if I had.

Regrets there are bound to be, because no one can get it right 100 per cent. But if regret remains regret or moves into remorse, it is profitless and even destructive.

I regret that I am flawed. I am flawed because I am human. God knows my flaws and failings. I have only to turn to him and ask for his freely offered help and companionship, and he forgives. He not only forgives but he makes all things new.

It is up to me to accept his forgiveness, to know that, flawed and failing, I am forgiven. It is up to me to put the cover on the duvet, saying, like Brother Lawrence, 'Without you I will always mess things up, but your grace is sufficient for me. Praise God.'

❖

Now there is no more doing. Hand and eye
Have lost their urgent creativity.
Now there is no more seeking of applause
For work or art or cause.
Simply the eyes seek affirmation of her being,
Waiting to answer smiling with a smile;
And holding eye and smile you sense the freeing,
Love and acceptance for her deepest soul.
'To see her,' people say, 'must be distressing',
And miss the blessing.[10]

NOTES

1. *Bloom Where You're Planted*, Carolyn Huffman (Word Books, 1976).
2. *Paths to Power*, A.W. Tozer (Marshall Morgan and Scott, 1972).
3. Quoted by Major Art Athens in a 1995 newsletter of the Officers' Christian Union.
4. *Chronicle of My Mother*, Yasushi Inoue (Konansha International, 1982).
5. *Sweet Adeline*, Patricia Slack and Frank Melville (Macmillan Education, 1988), p. 151.
6. *Mother's Song*, John Sherrill (Hodder and Stoughton, 1982).
7. *Into the Light*, Jocelyn Ryder-Smith (Radio 4, 31 January 1988).
8. Ibid.
9. 'Footprints', authorship disputed.
10. 'My mother in senility', Alexine Crawford, *Christian Poetry* (FCW, 1983).

GROWING A CARING CHURCH

PRACTICAL GUIDELINES FOR PASTORAL CARE

WENDY BILLINGTON

In every church, of every size, meeting people's pastoral needs is a core area of ministry. If leadership resources are already stretched, however, it can be an area in which it is all too easy to fall short, with potentially disastrous consequences. We may notice and feel compassion when we see somebody struggling in some way, but we also need to be properly equipped in order to offer the kind of wise and practical assistance that will start to guide them back towards wholeness of life.

Earthed in Jesus' command that as his disciples we are to love one another, this book shows how home groups can be places where people's pain and difficulties are noticed, and first steps taken to help. Writing for both group leaders and members, Wendy Billington offers valuable insights coupled with down-to-earth advice, drawing on her years of pastoral work in the community and in the local church, as well as on her personal experiences of loss and cancer.

ISBN 978 1 84101 799 0   £6.99